PARTY COOKING

Edited by
Jean Prince

Contents

Weights and Measures................................7

Introduction.................................8

Cocktail Savouries............................ 10

Party Drinks........................... 16

Buffet Parties.................................23

Dinner Parties..............................54

Children's Party...........................78

Christmas Celebration 86

Index......................................91

This edition first published 1980 by
Octopus Books Limited
59 Grosvenor Street, London W.1.

© 1980 Octopus Books Limited

ISBN 0 7064 1340 7

Produced and printed in Hong Kong by
Mandarin Publishers Limited
22a Westlands Road, Quarry Bay

Cover photography by Paul Williams

Frontispiece: FROSTED FRUITS *(page 90)*
(Photograph: The British Sugar Bureau)

Weights and Measures

All measurements in this book are given in Metric, Imperial and American.

Measurements in weight in the Imperial and American system are the same. Liquid measurements are different, and the following table shows the equivalents:

Liquid measurements

1 Imperial pint	20 fluid ounces
1 American pint	16 fluid ounces
1 American cup	8 fluid ounces

Level spoon measurements

1 tablespoon	15 ml
1 teaspoon	5 ml

Remember that the ingredients columns are not interchangeable. Follow only one set of measures.

INTRODUCTION

Giving a successful party is fun, but a common cry before the event is "What shall I serve?" If it is a dinner party there is the decision of what starter and dessert to put with the chosen main course. For buffet and lunch parties, children's birthday and festive dinner parties there is always the search for something new.

But from now on all you have to do is to decide what sort of party you are going to give. The rest I have done for you.

You will find delicious menus for all occasions. There's a romantic dinner for two, dinner parties for from four to eight, and small informal buffets and lunch parties for from 10 to 16, which include easy-to-prepare dishes that can be made in advance, with just a few last minute touches.

There is also a special occasion buffet which takes a little longer to prepare but is the ideal choice for an engagement, wedding, christening or anniversary celebration.

Children's parties are great fun to cater for and I have found that the basic formula for success is to provide lots of cakes and biscuits in a variety of shapes and textures, just a few sandwiches and plenty of savoury nibbles. If the children are very young, they will be happiest if you limit the number of guests to a maximum of eight and keep the party short, two hours at the most.

The Christmas celebration lunch has traditional turkey and accompaniments, followed by a spectacular meringue to delight and impress your family and guests. To make it even more of a special occasion, there is a table decoration of frosted fruits that looks fantastic but is surprisingly easy.

But before you begin any party preparation, invest a few pence in a hardback notebook to keep as your party planner. Write down your guest list and then list the chosen menu and work out quantities and a cooking timetable.

Make a note of the dishes that can be prepared in advance and put in your freezer. Spread your cooking over several days if possible and tick off the dishes on your list as you go.

For the day of the party, prepare a timetable. Write down the time when your guests are due to arrive and when you want to serve the meal. If you need to begin preparing food in the morning, write down what you plan to do at 11 a.m. and so on. And don't forget to plan in a snack lunch and time to get yourself ready. Writing everything down helps you to avoid last minute hitches and to be ready and smiling when guests arrive.

If you are a regular dinner party hostess, you will find that notebook also provides a useful record of the dishes you served. When the same guests next come to dinner, you won't be frantically trying to remember what you served them last time!

SEAFOOD WITH LEEKS *(page 55)* *(Photograph: The White Fish Kitchen)*

8

COCKTAIL SAVOURIES

Stuffed Eggs

METRIC/IMPERIAL
12 hard-boiled eggs
50 g/2 oz soft liver pâté
2 tablespoons thick mayonnaise
salt
freshly ground black pepper
To Garnish:
pimento-stuffed green olives, sliced

AMERICAN
12 hard-cooked eggs
$\frac{1}{4}$ cup soft liver pâté
2 tablespoons thick mayonnaise
salt
freshly ground black pepper
To Garnish:
pimento-stuffed green olives, sliced

Halve the eggs lengthwise, carefully remove the yolks and rub through a coarse sieve. Beat in the pâté and mayonnaise and season to taste with salt and black pepper.

Place the mixture in a piping (pastry) bag fitted with a small nozzle and pipe back into the egg whites. Garnish with sliced olives.

Cover and keep in the refrigerator until required.

Makes 24

Salmon and Prawn (Shrimp) Bouchées

METRIC/IMPERIAL

24 frozen bouchée cases (cocktail vol-au-vents)
1 egg yolk
25 g/1 oz margarine
25 g/1 oz plain flour
300 ml/½ pint milk
salt
freshly ground black pepper
1 × 210 g/7½ oz can salmon, drained
50 g/2 oz peeled prawns, chopped

AMERICAN

24 frozen bouchée cases (cocktail vol-au-vents)
1 egg yolk
2 tablespoons margarine
¼ cup all-purpose flour
1¼ cups milk
salt
freshly ground black pepper
1 × 7½ oz can salmon, drained
⅓ cup shelled shrimp, chopped

Arrange the bouchée cases on baking (cookie) sheets and brush the tops with egg yolk. Place in a preheated hot oven (230°C/450°F, Gas Mark 8) and cook until well risen and golden, about 10 to 15 minutes. Place on a wire rack and remove the pastry lids. Leave to cool, or keep warm.

Melt the margarine in a pan, add the flour and cook for 2 minutes. Gradually stir in the milk and bring to the boil, stirring. Cook for 2 minutes. Add salt and black pepper to taste. Turn the sauce into 2 bowls. Add the salmon to one half and the prawns (shrimp) to the other. Check the seasoning.

Spoon the sauces, hot or cold, into the pastry cases and replace the lids. Serve hot or cold.

Makes 24

Party Pinwheels

METRIC/IMPERIAL

175 g/6 oz cream cheese
1 × 198 g/7 oz can sweetcorn, drained
9 square slices of cooked packet ham, about 225 g/8 oz
1 × 425 g/15 oz can long asparagus spears, drained

AMERICAN

¾ cup cream cheese
1 × 7 oz can kernel corn, drained
9 square slices of processed package ham, about ½ lb
1 × 15 oz can long asparagus spears, drained

Beat together the cheese and corn until creamy, then spread over the slices of ham. Place one asparagus spear on one edge of each slice and then roll up. Chill well. Cut each roll into 3 pieces to serve.

Makes 27

Mexican Avocado Dip

METRIC/IMPERIAL
4 large ripe avocados
4 tablespoons lemon juice
1 Spanish onion, grated
150 ml/¼ pint mayonnaise
  (see page 50)
1 × 198 g/7 oz can sweetcorn with
  green pepper
salt
freshly ground black pepper
To Garnish:
chopped chives

AMERICAN
4 large ripe avocados
¼ cup lemon juice
1 Spanish onion, grated
⅔ cup mayonnaise (see page 50)
1 × 7 oz can kernel corn with green
  pepper
salt
freshly ground black pepper
To Garnish:
chopped chives

Halve and stone (pit) the avocados. Scoop out the flesh and mash well. Stir in the lemon juice, onion, mayonnaise and corn. Add salt and black pepper to taste.

Spoon into a serving dish and sprinkle with chives. Serve with savoury biscuits (crackers) and crisps.
Serves 12 to 16

Gruyère Moons

METRIC/IMPERIAL
175 g/6 oz plain flour
175 g/6 oz unsalted butter, softened
175 g/6 oz Gruyère cheese, grated
1 egg, beaten
salt
pinch of cayenne pepper
1 egg yolk to glaze

AMERICAN
1½ cups all-purpose flour
¾ cup sweet butter, softened
1½ cups grated Gruyère cheese
1 egg, beaten
salt
pinch of cayenne pepper
1 egg yolk to glaze

Blend together the flour and butter, then work in the cheese and egg. Add salt and cayenne pepper and blend thoroughly to make a soft dough. Sprinkle with flour and chill for at least 30 minutes.

Divide the dough in half; leave one portion in the refrigerator. Roll out the other half on a floured surface to 3 mm (⅛ inch) thickness. Cut into rounds using a 7.5 cm (3 inch) plain cutter, then cut into each circle to make a half-moon shape. Re-roll all the trimmings and re-cut until all the dough is used. Repeat with the remaining portion of dough.

Place on lightly greased baking (cookie) sheets and brush with egg yolk. Place in a preheated moderate oven (180°C/350°F, Gas Mark 4) and bake for 8 minutes. Serve warm or cold.
Makes 30

GRUYERE MOONS *(Photograph: Cheeses from Switzerland Ltd)*

Cheese Aigrettes

METRIC/IMPERIAL
40 g/1½ oz butter
150 ml/¼ pint water
65 g/2½ oz plain flour
2 eggs, beaten
Filling:
175 g/6 oz cream cheese
1 teaspoon lemon juice
little garlic powder
little milk (optional)
paprika

AMERICAN
3 tablespoons butter
⅓ cup water
½ cup + 2 tablespoons all-purpose
 flour
2 eggs, beaten
Filling:
¾ cup cream cheese
1 teaspoon lemon juice
little garlic powder
little milk (optional)
paprika

Melt the butter in the water in a small pan, then bring to the boil. Stir in the flour and beat until the mixture forms a ball in the centre of pan. Allow to cool slightly, then gradually beat in the eggs.

Spoon or pipe the mixture into 24 walnut-sized balls on 2 greased baking (cookie) sheets. Place in a preheated moderately hot oven (200°C/400°F, Gas Mark 6) and bake for 15 to 20 minutes until golden. Make a hole in the base of each, then cool on a wire rack.

Cream the cheese with the lemon juice and garlic powder to taste; add a little milk if necessary to make a soft mixture. Place in a piping (pastry) bag fitted with a small nozzle and pipe into each bun at the base. Serve sprinkled with paprika.
Makes 24

Party Kebabs

METRIC/IMPERIAL
triangles of Edam cheese
black grapes, seeded
stuffed olives
squares of green pepper
slices of salami, halved and rolled up
mandarin orange segments
maraschino cherries

AMERICAN
triangles of Edam cheese
purple grapes, pipped
stuffed olives
squares of green pepper
slices of salami, halved and rolled up
mandarin orange segments
maraschino cherries

Thread all the ingredients alternately onto cocktail sticks (toothpicks) or skewers. Stick into a red cabbage to serve.

Cheese Twists

METRIC/IMPERIAL
1 × 225 g/8 oz packet shortcrust
  pastry mix
75 g/3 oz Cheddar cheese, finely
  grated
$\frac{1}{2}$ teaspoon mustard powder
salt
freshly ground black pepper
paprika

AMERICAN
1 × $\frac{1}{2}$ lb package basic pie dough mix
$\frac{3}{4}$ cup finely grated Cheddar cheese
$\frac{1}{2}$ teaspoon mustard powder
salt
freshly ground black pepper
paprika

Mix together the shortcrust pastry (basic pie dough) mix, cheese, mustard and salt and black pepper to taste. Add enough cold water to form a firm dough, draw together and knead lightly. Turn onto a floured board and roll out to a rectangle 30 × 25 cm (12 × 10 inches). Cut into strips 10 cm (4 inches) long and 5 mm ($\frac{1}{4}$ inch) wide.

Twist two strips of pastry (dough) together, sealing the ends well, and place on a baking (cookie) sheet. Repeat until all the pastry (dough) is used. Place in a preheated moderately hot oven (200°C/400°F, Gas Mark 6) and bake for 10 to 15 minutes until golden brown. Cool on a wire rack then dip the ends in paprika.

Makes approximately 70 cheese twists

PARTY DRINKS

Hot Spiced Ginger Cup

METRIC/IMPERIAL	AMERICAN
4 small cooking apples, each studded with 5 cloves	4 small baking apples, each studded with 5 cloves
2 tablespoons demerara sugar	2 tablespoons brown sugar
1 orange, sliced	1 orange, sliced
2 cinnamon sticks	2 cinnamon sticks
4 × 960 ml/32.5 fl oz bottles dry cider	6 pints hard cider
1 miniature bottle dark rum	1 miniature bottle dark rum

Place the apples in a pan with the sugar, orange slices and cinnamon. Just cover with cider and simmer for 5 minutes. Remove the cinnamon and add the rum and remaining cider. Bring to the boil then pour into a heatproof punch bowl and serve hot.
Serves 24

Fruity Ginger Cup

METRIC/IMPERIAL	AMERICAN
450 ml/$\frac{3}{4}$ pint tea liquor (see below)	2 cups tea liquor (see below)
600 ml/1 pint sparkling apple juice	$2\frac{1}{2}$ cups sparkling apple juice
600 ml/1 pint grape juice	$2\frac{1}{2}$ cups grape juice
600 ml/1 pint ginger ale	$2\frac{1}{2}$ cups ginger ale
4 tablespoons lime juice cordial	$\frac{1}{4}$ cup lime juice cordial
4 tablespoons clear honey	$\frac{1}{4}$ cup clear honey
To Garnish:	**To Garnish:**
ice cubes	ice cubes
12 lemon slices	12 lemon slices
12 cocktail cherries	12 cocktail cherries

Put all the ingredients in a glass jug or fruit bowl and stir well. Add ice cubes, and lemon slices and cocktail cherries speared together on cocktail sticks (toothpicks). Add one to each glass when serving.

To make tea liquor: Put 25 g/1 oz dry tea into 600 ml/1 pint/$2\frac{1}{2}$ cups cold water and leave overnight. Strain off the liquid and use as required.
Serves 12

FRUITY GINGER CUP *(Photograph: The Tea Council)*

Strawberry Wine Cup

METRIC/IMPERIAL	AMERICAN
100 g/4 oz whole strawberries	*1 cup whole strawberries*
1 bottle white wine	*1 bottle white wine*
2 tablespoons brandy	*2 tablespoons brandy*
1.2 litres/2 pints lemonade	*5 cups lemonade*
To Garnish:	**To Garnish:**
mint sprigs	*mint sprigs*

Place the strawberries in a serving bowl and pour over the wine and brandy. Chill for 1 hour. Just before serving, pour in the lemonade and garnish with mint.

Serves 10

Mulled Wine

METRIC/IMPERIAL	AMERICAN
600 ml/1 pint water	*$2\frac{1}{2}$ cups water*
225 g/8 oz sugar	*1 cup sugar*
6 whole cloves	*6 whole cloves*
$\frac{1}{2}$ a cinnamon stick	*$\frac{1}{2}$ a cinnamon stick*
4 lemons, sliced	*4 lemons, sliced*
2 bottles red wine	*2 bottles red wine*
To Garnish:	**To Garnish:**
1 orange, thinly sliced	*1 orange, thinly sliced*

Place the water, sugar, cloves and cinnamon in a pan and heat gently, stirring until the sugar is dissolved. Bring to the boil; add the lemon slices and leave to stand for 15 minutes. Add the wine and heat through gently; do *not* allow to boil.

Strain into a serving bowl and garnish with orange slices.

Serves 12

Summer Sunset Punch

METRIC/IMPERIAL	AMERICAN
1 bottle Reisling	1 bottle Reisling
1 bottle Beaujolais	1 bottle Beaujolais
450 ml/¾ pint tea liquor (see Fruity Ginger Cup)	2 cups tea liquor (see Fruity Ginger Cup)
soda water	soda water
To Garnish:	**To Garnish:**
12 lime slices	12 lime slices
½ small melon, cut into 12 squares	½ small melon, cut into 12 squares
ice cubes	ice cubes

Place the wines and tea liquor in a glass jug and stir well. Add soda water to taste, and a slice of lime and a melon cube speared together on a cocktail stick (toothpick). Garnish each glass with one stick of speared lime and melon to serve and add ice as required.
Serves 12

Chilled Tomato Cocktail

METRIC/IMPERIAL	AMERICAN
1 × 396 g/14 oz can tomato juice	1 × 14 oz can tomato juice
juice of 1 lemon	juice of 1 lemon
1 tablespoon Worcestershire sauce	1 tablespoon Worcestershire sauce
pinch of salt	pinch of salt
½ teaspoon made mustard	½ teaspoon prepared mustard
4 tablespoons medium sherry	¼ cup medium sherry
To Garnish:	**To Garnish:**
strips of cucumber rind	strips of cucumber rind

Place the can of tomato juice in the refrigerator until well chilled. Mix the remaining ingredients together, add the tomato juice and stir well.

Rub the rims of 4 small glasses with a piece of lemon then dip in sugar to coat 1 cm/½ inch deep; shake off surplus sugar.

Pour the cocktail into the glasses and garnish with the cucumber rind. Leave in the refrigerator until required.
Serves 4

Rum Cola

METRIC/IMPERIAL
1.2 litres/2 pints cola, chilled
600 ml/1 pint diluted orange squash
300 ml/$\frac{1}{2}$ pint white rum
To Garnish:
ice cubes
10 orange slices

AMERICAN
5 cups cola, chilled
2$\frac{1}{2}$ cups diluted orange squash
1 cup white rum
To Garnish:
ice cubes
10 orange slices

Mix all the ingredients together in a bowl. Add ice cubes and orange slices and serve at once.
Serves 10

Variation: Lemon Gin

METRIC/IMPERIAL
1.25 litres/2$\frac{1}{4}$ pints bitter lemon
600 ml/1 pint diluted lemon squash
300 ml/$\frac{1}{2}$ pint gin
To Garnish:
ice cubes
10 lemon slices

AMERICAN
5$\frac{3}{4}$ cups bitter lemon
2$\frac{1}{2}$ cups diluted lemon squash
1 cup gin
To Garnish:
ice cubes
10 lemon slices

Make as above.
Serves 10

Dubonnet Punch

METRIC/IMPERIAL
1 × 411 g/14$\frac{1}{2}$ oz can fruit cocktail
4 tablespoons brandy
1 bottle Dubonnet
2 × 326 ml/11.5 fl oz cans lemonade
To Garnish:
orange and lemon slices
ice cubes

AMERICAN
1 × 14$\frac{1}{2}$ oz can fruit cocktail
$\frac{1}{4}$ cup brandy
1 bottle Dubonnet
2$\frac{3}{4}$ cups lemonade
To Garnish:
orange and lemon slices
ice cubes

Place the fruit cocktail, with its syrup, in a serving bowl, add the brandy and leave for several hours. Add the Dubonnet and lemonade and mix well. Float orange and lemon slices on the surface, add ice and serve.
Serves 10

From top left, clockwise: DUBONNET PUNCH, MOULIN ROUGE
and CIDER ORANGE CUP *(page 22),* LEMON GIN
(Photograph: The Tea Council)

Moulin Rouge

METRIC/IMPERIAL
For each glass:
2–3 ice cubes
1 measure of Dubonnet
150 ml/¼ pint lemonade
To Garnish:
spiral of lemon rind

AMERICAN
For each glass:
2–3 ice cubes
1 measure of Dubonnet
⅔ cup lemonade
To Garnish:
spiral of lemon rind

Put the ice and Dubonnet in a glass jug and pour the lemonade over. Serve in tall glasses, garnished with lemon rind.

Cider Orange Cup

METRIC/IMPERIAL
750 ml/1¼ pints orange juice
ice
1 litre/1¾ pints cider
600 ml/1 pint water
To Garnish:
cucumber and orange slices

AMERICAN
3 cups orange juice
ice
4¼ cups cider
2½ cups water
To Garnish:
cucumber and orange slices ·

Place all the ingredients in a glass serving bowl and mix well together. Float the cucumber and orange slices on the surface.
Serves 10

Sherry Sangaree

METRIC/IMPERIAL
For each glass:
½ teaspoon castor sugar
2 fl oz medium dry sherry
sprinkle nutmeg
To Garnish:
slice of lemon or lime

AMERICAN
For each glass:
½ teaspoon sugar
2 oz medium dry sherry
sprinkle nutmeg
To Garnish:
slice of lemon or lime

Mix the sugar, sherry and nutmeg until sugar is almost dissolved. Place ice cubes in a small tumbler and pour sherry mixture over. Garnish with slice of lemon or lime and serve.

BUFFET PARTIES

BUFFET FOR 10

Tomato and Prawn (Shrimp) Starter

Cheese Fondue   Turkey Provençal

Fresh Fruit Flan
or
Orange Cheesecake

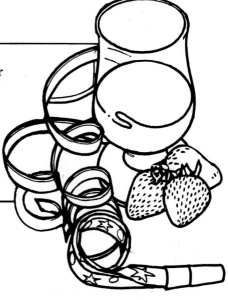

Cheese Fondue

METRIC/IMPERIAL
1 clove garlic, skinned
750 g/1½ lb Emmental cheese, grated
750 g/1½ lb Gruyère cheese, grated
1½ tablespoons plain flour
1 bottle dry white wine
2 teaspoons lemon juice
freshly ground black pepper
To Serve:
2 French loaves, cubed

AMERICAN
1 garlic clove, skinned
6 cups grated Emmental cheese
6 cups grated Gruyère cheese
1½ tablespoons all-purpose flour
1 bottle dry white wine
2 teaspoons lemon juice
freshly ground black pepper
To Serve:
2 French loaves, cubed

Rub the garlic around a large fondue pot; discard garlic. Place the cheeses, flour, wine and lemon juice in the pot and bring quickly to the boil, stirring all the time. Add pepper to taste. Place over a low heat on a fondue burner.

To serve, the guests place a cube of bread on a skewer and dip it into the fondue.

Tomato and Prawn (Shrimp) Starter

METRIC/IMPERIAL
20 medium firm tomatoes, skinned
350 g/12 oz peeled prawns
4 sticks celery, finely chopped
2 dessert apples, cored and chopped
2 avocados, peeled and diced
1 green pepper, cored, seeded and
  finely chopped
1 tablespoon lemon juice
1 × 284 ml/10 fl oz carton soured
  cream
salt
freshly ground black pepper
To Garnish:
parsley sprigs

AMERICAN
20 medium firm tomatoes, skinned
2 cups shelled shrimp
4 celery stalks, finely chopped
2 dessert apples, cored and chopped
2 avocados, peeled and diced
1 green pepper, cored, seeded and
  finely chopped
1 tablespoon lemon juice
$1\frac{1}{4}$ cups sour cream
salt
freshly ground black pepper
To Garnish:
parsley sprigs

Cut off the rounded end of the tomatoes and carefully scoop out the insides with a teaspoon.

Chop the tomato pulp and mix with the prawns (shrimp), celery, apple, avocado, green pepper and lemon juice. Toss lightly together.

Stir in the cream and season well with salt and black pepper. Season the insides of the tomatoes, then spoon in the filling.

Replace the lids and arrange on a serving dish garnished with parsley.

CHEESE FONDUE *(page 23) (Photograph: Cheeses from Switzerland Ltd)*

24

Turkey Provençal

METRIC/IMPERIAL	AMERICAN
5 large boned turkey breasts, skinned	5 large boneless turkey breasts, skinned
150 ml/¼ pint white wine	⅔ cup white wine
450 ml/¾ pint chicken stock	2 cups chicken bouillon
1 medium onion	1 medium onion
pinch of thyme	pinch of thyme
1 bay leaf	1 bay leaf
few parsley stalks	few parsley stalks
Vegetable sauce:	**Vegetable sauce:**
2 tablespoons oil	2 tablespoons oil
25 g/1 oz butter	2 tablespoons butter
3 onions, sliced	3 onions, sliced
350 g/12 oz courgettes, sliced	¾ lb zucchini, sliced
225 g/8 oz button mushrooms, sliced	2 cups sliced button mushrooms
10 tomatoes, skinned, seeded and chopped	10 tomatoes, skinned, seeded and chopped
pinch of mixed herbs	pinch of mixed herbs
salt	salt
freshly ground black pepper	freshly ground black pepper
Topping:	**Topping:**
1 kg/2 lb potatoes, cooked and mashed	4 cups mashed potato
225 g/8 oz Cheddar cheese, grated	2 cups grated Cheddar cheese

Place the turkey breasts, wine, stock (bouillon), whole onion, thyme, bay leaf and parsley in a pan. Bring to the boil, then cook gently until the turkey is tender, 30 to 40 minutes. Remove the turkey, cut into slices and keep warm. Strain the cooking liquid and reserve 150 ml/¼ pint/⅔ cup. [Use the leftover stock (bouillon) for soup].

To prepare the sauce: Heat the oil and butter in a frying pan (skillet) and fry the onions and courgettes (zucchini) until soft. Add the remaining ingredients with salt and black pepper to taste, and the reserved stock (bouillon), and cook until tender, about 10 to 15 minutes.

Place alternate layers of sliced turkey and vegetables in an ovenproof dish.

Mix the potato and cheese together and place in a piping (pastry) bag fitted with a star nozzle. Pipe an attractive pattern over the top and place under a preheated grill (broiler) until browned.

Note: the topping could be prepared in advance, without browning, and heated through in a preheated moderate oven (180°C/350°F, Gas Mark 4) for about 1 hour until hot and golden.

Orange Cheesecake

METRIC/IMPERIAL

2 tablespoons syrup
2 tablespoons cocoa powder
50 g/2 oz butter
225 g/8 oz wholewheat biscuits,
  crushed

Filling:

2 oranges
1 lemon
orange juice or squash
15 g/½ oz gelatine
100 g/4 oz caster sugar
500 g/1 lb cottage cheese
1 × 142 ml/5 fl oz carton double
  cream, whipped

To Decorate:

grated chocolate

AMERICAN

2 tablespoons maple syrup
2 tablespoons unsweetened cocoa
¼ cup butter
3 cups Graham Cracker crumbs

Filling:

2 oranges
1 lemon
orange juice or squash
2 envelopes gelatin
½ cup superfine sugar
1 × 1 lb carton ricotta cheese
⅔ cup heavy cream, whipped

To Decorate:

grated chocolate

Place the syrup, cocoa and butter in a saucepan over a gentle heat until the mixture thickens, stirring occasionally. Add the biscuit (cracker) crumbs and mix well. Spread the mixture over the base of a 25 cm/10 inch loose-based flan tin (pie pan) and press down firmly. Place in the refrigerator to set.

Grate the rind and squeeze the juice from the oranges and lemon and place in a measuring jug. Make up to 300 ml/½ pint/1¼ cups with orange juice or squash. Place the gelatine (gelatin) in a bowl with 5 tablespoons water, place over a pan of simmering water and stir until dissolved. Add to the juice with the sugar, stirring until dissolved.

Place the cheese in an electric blender or rub through a coarse sieve until smooth. Add to the fruit juice.

Stir the cream into the cheese mixture and blend thoroughly until really smooth; if necessary, whisk for a few minutes with an electric hand whisk.

Pour over the biscuit (cracker) base and place in the refrigerator for a few hours until set.

Carefully place the cheesecake on a serving plate and sprinkle with chocolate.

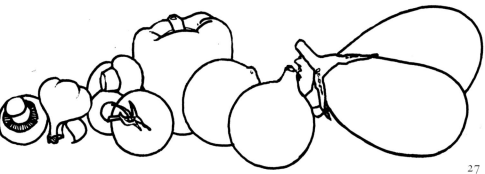

Fresh Fruit Flan

METRIC/IMPERIAL

All-in-one pastry:
150 g/5 oz soft margarine
2 tablespoons water
225 g/8 oz plain flour

Filling:
25 g/1 oz butter
4 teaspoons plain flour
120 ml/4 fl oz milk
25 g/1 oz caster sugar
1 egg yolk
1 tablespoon single cream
1 tablespoon sherry
1 × 312 g/11 oz can mandarin
    oranges
100 g/4 oz black grapes, halved and
    seeded
50 g/2 oz cherries, halved and stoned
1 banana, sliced
1 teaspoon arrowroot

AMERICAN

All-in-one pastry:
$\frac{5}{8}$ cup soft margarine
2 tablespoons water
2 cups all-purpose flour

Filling:
2 tablespoons butter
4 teaspoons all-purpose flour
$\frac{1}{2}$ cup milk
2 tablespoons sugar
1 egg yolk
1 tablespoon light cream
1 tablespoon sherry
1 × 11 oz can mandarin oranges
1 cup halved and pitted purple
    grapes
$\frac{1}{2}$ cup halved and stoned cherries
1 banana, sliced
1 teaspoon arrowroot

To make the pastry: Place the margarine in a large bowl, add the water and 2 tablespoons of the flour and beat with a fork for 30 seconds until well blended. Stir in the remaining flour and mix to a firm dough. Knead lightly on a floured surface, roll out and use to line a 23 cm/9 inch fluted flan tin (pie pan). Prick the base with a fork, line with greased greaseproof (waxed) paper, fill with dried beans and bake blind in a preheated moderately hot oven (200°C/400°F, Gas Mark 6) for 20 minutes. Remove the paper and beans and return to the oven for 5 minutes. Allow to cool.

To make the filling: Melt the butter in a saucepan, add the flour and cook for 2 minutes, stirring. Gradually add the milk and bring to the boil, stirring continuously. Remove from the heat, cool slightly, then beat in the sugar, egg yolk, cream and sherry.

Place the flan case on a serving plate and pour in the custard; smooth the surface. Leave to set.

Drain the mandarin oranges, reserving the syrup, and arrange the fruits in alternate circles on the custard, finishing with a grape in the centre.

Blend the arrowroot with 150 ml/$\frac{1}{4}$ pint/$\frac{2}{3}$ cup of the reserved syrup (made up with water if necessary) and bring to the boil, stirring continuously. Cool slightly, then spoon over the fruit and leave to set. Serve cold with pouring cream.

TOMATO AND PRAWN (SHRIMP) STARTER *(page 24)*
(Photograph: Fyffes Group)

LUNCH PARTY FOR 12

Lambs' Liver Pâté
Warm French Bread

Mushroom and Chicken Tarts
Tuna and Cheese Flan
Waldorf Salad
Tomato and Onion Salad

Black Forest Cherry Gâteau
Fruit Salad

Lambs' Liver Pâté

METRIC/IMPERIAL
350 g/6 oz butter
500 g/1 lb lambs' liver, chopped
350 g/12 oz streaky bacon, derinded
  and chopped
2 medium onions, finely chopped
2 cloves garlic, crushed
2 bay leaves
4–6 tablespoons brandy or sherry
salt
freshly ground black pepper
To Garnish:
parsley sprigs

AMERICAN
¾ cup butter
1 lb lamb liver, chopped
1½ cups chopped fatty bacon slices
2 medium onions, finely chopped
2 garlic cloves, minced
2 bay leaves
4–6 tablespoons brandy or sherry
salt
freshly ground black pepper
To Garnish:
parsley sprigs

Melt 150 g/5 oz/⅝ cup of the butter in a frying pan (skillet), add the liver, bacon, onion, garlic and bay leaves, cover and fry gently for 15 minutes. Remove the bay leaves and put the mixture twice through a fine mincer (grinder).

Add the brandy or sherry, salt and black pepper to taste, and beat well. Turn into a serving dish. Melt the remaining butter and pour over the top to seal the surface. Chill well.

Garnish with parsley to serve.

Tuna and Cheese Flan

METRIC/IMPERIAL

1 × 500 g/1 lb packet shortcrust
  pastry mix
2 × 198 g/7 oz cans tuna fish
1 large onion, sliced
175 g/6 oz Cheddar cheese, grated
pinch of salt
1½ teaspoons paprika
3 eggs, beaten
450 ml/¾ pint milk
To Garnish:
cucumber slices
parsley sprig

AMERICAN

1 × 1 lb package basic pie dough
2 × 7 oz cans tuna fish
1 large onion, sliced
1½ cups grated Cheddar cheese
pinch of salt
1½ teaspoons paprika
3 eggs, beaten
2 cups milk
To Garnish:
cucumber slices
parsley sprig

Make up pastry (dough) mix according to packet (package) instructions. Roll out on a floured board and use to line a 23 cm/12 inch fluted French flan tin (pie pan). Bake blind (see Mushroom and Chicken Tarts) in a preheated moderately hot oven (190°C/375°F, Gas Mark 5) for 15 minutes.

Drain the oil from the tuna and place the oil in a saucepan. Add the onion and fry until tender, then transfer to the flan case. Flake the tuna and spread over the onion. Sprinkle the cheese over the top and season with salt and paprika.

Whisk the eggs and milk together, then pour into the flan case. Return to the oven for about 50 minutes until golden and firm. Leave to cool.

Place on a serving plate and garnish with cucumber and parsley to serve.

Mushroom and Chicken Tarts

METRIC/IMPERIAL	AMERICAN
275 g/10 oz shortcrust pastry mix	2½ cups basic pie dough mix
25 g/1 oz butter	2 tablespoons butter
1 small onion, finely chopped	1 small onion, finely chopped
50 g/2 oz mushrooms, finely chopped	½ cup finely chopped mushrooms
25 g/1 oz plain flour	¼ cup all-purpose flour
300 ml/½ pint milk	1¼ cups milk
100 g/4 oz cooked chicken, diced	½ cup diced cooked chicken
1 stick celery, finely chopped	1 celery stalk, finely chopped
salt	salt
freshly ground black pepper	freshly ground black pepper
To Garnish:	**To Garnish:**
strips of canned pimento	strips of canned pimento

Make up pastry (dough) mix according to packet (package) instructions. Roll out on a floured surface and use to line 12 deep patty tins (muffin pans). Cover each base with greased greaseproof (waxed) paper, fill with dried beans and bake blind in a preheated hot oven (220°C/425°F, Gas Mark 7) for 10 minutes. Remove the paper and beans and return to the oven for 5 minutes. Cool on a wire rack or keep warm.

Melt the butter in a frying pan (skillet), add the onion and fry until tender. Stir in the mushrooms and cook for 1 minute. Stir in the flour and cook for 1 minute. Remove from the heat and gradually stir in the milk, then bring to boil, stirring, and cook for 1 minute. Add the chicken, celery and salt and black pepper to taste. Heat gently, if serving warm, or leave to cool.

Arrange the pastry cases on a serving plate, spoon in the filling and decorate with pimento.

From top left, clockwise: BLACK FOREST CHERRY GATEAU *(page 35),* HOT SPICED CIDER CUP *(page 16),* WALDORF SALAD and TOMATO AND ONION SALAD *(page 34),* TUNA AND CHEESE FLAN *(page 31),* FRUIT SALAD *(page 34)* and MUSHROOM AND CHICKEN TARTS *(Photograph: The Home Baking Bureau*

Tomato and Onion Salad

METRIC/IMPERIAL
1 kg/2 lb tomatoes, sliced
2 large onions, sliced
2 teaspoons caster sugar
2 tablespoons French dressing

AMERICAN
2 lb tomatoes, sliced
2 large onions, sliced
2 teaspoons superfine sugar
2 tablespoons French dressing

Arrange the tomatoes and onions in a salad dish, sprinkle with the sugar and pour over the dressing. Cover with cling film (saran wrap) and place in the refrigerator until required.

Waldorf Salad

METRIC/IMPERIAL
1 white cabbage, shredded
1 head of celery, cut into 2.5 cm/1 inch pieces
4 red dessert apples, quartered
100 g/4 oz raisins
50 g/2 oz walnut halves
1 × 225 g/8 oz bottle salad cream

AMERICAN
1 white cabbage, finely sliced
1 head of celery, cut into 1 inch pieces
4 red dessert apples, quartered
$\frac{3}{4}$ cup raisins
$\frac{1}{2}$ cup walnut halves
1 × $\frac{1}{2}$ lb bottle salad cream

Place all the ingredients in a large salad bowl and toss well. Cover with cling film (saran wrap) and place in the refrigerator until required.

Fruit Salad

METRIC/IMPERIAL
1 × 425 g/15 oz can peach slices
1 × 425 g/15 oz can pear halves
1 × 198 g/7 oz can stoned red cherries
1 small pineapple
2 tablespoons Kirsch (optional)
2 bananas

AMERICAN
1 × 15 oz can peach slices
1 × 15 oz can pear halves
1 × 7 oz can pitted red cherries
1 small pineapple
2 tablespoons Kirsch (optional)
2 bananas

Empty the cans of fruit and their juice into a large serving bowl. Cut the pineapple in half lengthways, remove the flesh and cut into 2.5 cm/1 inch pieces, removing the central core. Add to the bowl with the Kirsch (if using). Cover with cling film (saran wrap) and chill in the refrigerator. Just before serving, slice the bananas and stir into the fruit salad. Serve with pouring cream.

Black Forest Cherry Gâteau

METRIC/IMPERIAL
2 × 225 g/8 oz packets sponge mix
50 g/2 oz cocoa powder
2 eggs
120 ml/4 fl oz water
1 × 284 ml/10 fl oz carton double
cream, whipped
2 × 425 g/15 oz cans black cherries
drained and stoned
To Decorate:
chocolate vermicelli

AMERICAN
2 × ½ lb packages sponge mix
½ cup unsweetened cocoa
2 eggs
½ cup water
1¼ cups heavy cream, whipped
2 × 15 oz cans bing cherries, drained
and pitted
To Decorate:
chocolate vermicelli

Mix the sponge mix and cocoa together in a bowl, then whisk in the eggs and water as directed on the packet. Turn into 2 lined and greased 20 cm/8 inch sandwich tins (layer cake pans), place in a preheated moderate oven (180°C/350°F, Gas Mark 4) and bake for 30 to 35 minutes until risen and firm to touch. Turn onto a wire rack to cool.

Slice both cakes horizontally in half. Place one slice on a serving plate and cover with a layer of cream. Reserve 6 cherries for decoration, then arrange a third of the remaining cherries on top of the cream. Top with another slice of cake, spread with cream and top with half of the remaining cherries. Top with another slice of cake, spread with cream and arrange the last of the cherries on top.

Place the remaining slice of cake on top and cover thickly with cream. Use the rest of the cream to pipe 6 large swirls around the edge of the gâteau. Top each swirl with a cherry and sprinkle chocolate vermicelli in the centre.

BUFFET FOR 16

Soured Cream Mushrooms
Smoked Mackerel Pâté

Beef Olives with Horseradish
Boiled Rice
Green Salad with Vinaigrette Dressing

Strawberry Cheesecake

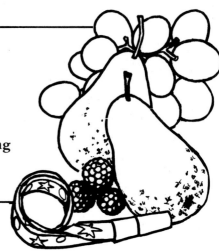

Soured Cream Mushrooms

METRIC/IMPERIAL
4 × 210 g/7½ oz cans small whole
  mushrooms in brine, drained
4 tablespoons mayonnaise
1 × 284 ml/10 fl oz carton soured
  cream
2 tablespoons dried tarragon
salt
freshly ground black pepper
To Garnish:
lettuce leaves
chopped parsley

AMERICAN
4 × 7½ oz cans small whole
  mushrooms in brine, drained
¼ cup mayonnaise
1¼ cups sour cream
2 tablespoons dried tarragon
salt
freshly ground black pepper
To Garnish:
lettuce leaves
chopped parsley

Mix together the mushrooms, mayonnaise, cream, tarragon and salt and
black pepper to taste. Place one or two lettuce leaves on individual
plates, top with the mushrooms and sprinkle with parsley.
Serves 8

SOURED CREAM MUSHROOMS *(Photograph: The Canned
Food Advisory Service)*

Smoked Mackerel Pâté

METRIC/IMPERIAL
500 g/1 lb smoked mackerel, flaked
1 × 142 ml/5 fl oz carton soured
  cream
500 g/16 oz carton cottage cheese,
  sieved
25 g/1 oz butter, melted
grated rind and juice of ½ lemon
salt
freshly ground black pepper

AMERICAN
1 lb smoked mackerel, flaked
⅔ cup sour cream
1 × 1 lb carton ricotta cheese, sieved
2 tablespoons butter, melted
grated rind and juice of ½ lemon
salt
freshly ground black pepper

Place the mackerel in an electric blender. Add the cream and cheese and blend until smooth. Stir in the butter, lemon rind and juice, and salt and black pepper to taste. Turn into one large dish or individual dishes. Serve with brown bread.
Serves 8

Beef Olives with Horseradish

METRIC/IMPERIAL
350 g/12 oz fresh breadcrumbs
175 g/6 oz shredded suet
4 tablespoons chopped parsley
120 ml/4 fl oz horseradish relish
salt
freshly ground black pepper
3 eggs, lightly beaten
32 thin slices top side of beef,
* trimmed of fat*
dripping or lard for frying
4 onions, chopped
1.75 litres/3 pints beef stock
4 tablespoons plain flour, blended
* with 120 ml/4 fl oz water,*
* (optional)*
To Garnish:
parsley sprigs

AMERICAN
6 cups fresh bread crumbs
1⅕ cups shredded suet
4 tablespoons chopped parsley
½ cup horseradish relish
salt
freshly ground black pepper
3 eggs, lightly beaten
32 thin slices top round of beef,
* trimmed of fat*
drippings or lard for frying
4 onions, chopped
7½ cups beef bouillon
¼ cup all-purpose flour blended with
* ½ cup water (optional)*
To Garnish:
parsley sprigs

Mix together the breadcrumbs, suet, chopped parsley, horseradish and salt and black pepper to taste. Add enough beaten egg to bind the mixture together. Divide the stuffing between the meat slices, roll up and secure with fine string or cocktail sticks (toothpicks).

Melt a little fat in a frying pan (skillet), add the beef olives in batches and brown well all over. Transfer to 1 or 2 casserole dishes as they brown; add more fat to the pan as necessary. Sprinkle the onions over the top and pour over the hot stock (bouillon). Cover and cook in a preheated moderate oven (160°C/325°F, Gas Mark 3) for 1½ to 2 hours until tender.

Strain off the liquid and thicken with the blended flour if desired.

Remove the string or cocktail sticks (toothpicks) from the beef olives, arrange on 2 serving dishes and pour over the sauce. Garnish with parsley sprigs.

Green Salad with Vinaigrette Dressing

METRIC/IMPERIAL

3 lettuce
3 bunches of watercress
3 heads of chicory, sliced
2 green peppers, cored, seeded and
  sliced
1 cucumber, sliced
Vinaigrette Dressing:
600 ml/1 pint salad oil
2 teaspoons dry mustard
1 teaspoon French mustard
salt
freshly ground black pepper
1 tablespoon sugar
300 ml/½ pint wine or cider vinegar
2 cloves garlic, crushed
1 onion, finely chopped
1 tablespoon mixed chopped fresh
  herbs

AMERICAN

3 heads of lettuce
3 bunches of watercress
3 heads of Belgian endive, sliced
2 green peppers, cored, seeded and
  sliced
1 cucumber, sliced
Vinaigrette Dressing:
2½ cups salad oil
2 teaspoons dry mustard
1 teaspoon French mustard
salt
freshly ground black pepper
1 tablespoon sugar
1¼ cups wine or cider vinegar
2 garlic cloves, minced
1 onion, finely chopped
1 tablespoon mixed chopped fresh
  herbs

Place the prepared salad ingredients in a salad bowl.

Put the dressing ingredients in a screw-top jar and shake well to blend.

Pour the dressing over the salad and toss well to coat, or serve separately.

BEEF OLIVES WITH HORSERADISH *(page 39)*
(Photograph: Frank Cooper)

Strawberry Cheesecake

METRIC/IMPERIAL

225 g/8 oz digestive biscuits, crushed
100 g/4 oz margarine, melted

Filling:
500 g/1 lb curd or cottage cheese,
  sieved
100 g/4 oz caster sugar
grated rind of 1 lemon
1 large egg, beaten
25 g/1 oz sultanas
milk to glaze

To Decorate:
1 × 142 ml/5 fl oz carton double
  cream, whipped
punnet of strawberries

AMERICAN

1½ cups crushed Graham crackers
½ cup margarine, melted

Filling:
1 × 1 lb carton curd or ricotta cheese,
  sieved
½ cup sugar
grated rind of 1 lemon
1 large egg, beaten
3 tablespoons seedless white raisins
milk to glaze

To Decorate:
⅔ cup heavy cream, whipped
punnet of strawberries

Mix together the crumbs and margarine. Press onto the bottom and sides of a greased 20 cm/8 inch flan dish (pie pan). Chill until firm.

Place the filling ingredients in a bowl and beat well for 1 to 2 minutes. Place in the crumb crust and brush with milk. Place in the centre of a preheated moderately hot oven (190°C/375°F, Gas Mark 5) and bake for 40 to 45 minutes or until firm. Leave to cool, then decorate with piped whipped cream and strawberries to serve.
Serves 8

BUFFET FOR 25

Smoked Haddock Mousse
Melba Toast

Party Quiche   Pineapple Chicken
Chicken Drumsticks en Croûte

Tomato Surprises   Rice Salad
Mixed Salad
Mayonnaise

Red Fruit Jelly   Profiteroles

Smoked Haddock Mousse

METRIC/IMPERIAL	AMERICAN
1.5 kg/3 lb smoked haddock	3 lb smoked haddock
milk	milk
40 g/1½ oz gelatine	6 envelopes gelatin
6 tablespoons lemon juice	6 tablespoons lemon juice
450 ml/¾ pint single cream	2 cups light cream
3 tablespoons horseradish relish	3 tablespoons horseradish relish
6 eggs, separated	6 eggs, separated
salt	salt
white pepper	white pepper
To Garnish:	**To Garnish:**
parsley sprigs	parsley sprigs
lemon wedges	lemon wedges

Remove the tail and any fins from the haddock. If necessary, cut the fish into pieces. Place in a large saucepan, just cover with milk and cook gently until tender, about 10 minutes. Remove the skin and bones and allow to cool.

Meanwhile, place the gelatine (gelatin) and lemon juice in a bowl over a pan of hot water and stir until dissolved.

Flake the fish into a bowl and add the cream, horseradish relish, egg yolks, gelatine (gelatin) and salt and pepper to taste.

Whisk the egg whites until stiff and fold into the fish mixture. Pour into 3 wetted 1.2 litre/2 pint/5 cup moulds and leave to set in the refrigerator.

Turn out onto serving plates and garnish with parsley and lemon wedges.

Melba Toast

2 thin-sliced white loaves

Cut the slices of bread in half diagonally. Place on baking (cookie) sheets and leave in a very cool oven (120°C/250°F, Gas Mark ½) for about 1½ hours until lightly coloured and crisp.

Party Quiche

METRIC/IMPERIAL	AMERICAN
400 g/14 oz plain flour	*3½ cups all-purpose flour*
pinch of salt	*pinch of salt*
200 g/7 oz butter or margarine	*⅞ cup butter or margarine*
2 large eggs, beaten with 4 tablespoons water	*2 large eggs, beaten with ¼ cup water*
Filling:	**Filling:**
8 large eggs	*8 large eggs*
1 × 284 ml/10 fl oz carton double cream	*1¼ cups heavy cream*
300 ml/½ pint milk	*1¼ cups milk*
2 × 326 g/11½ oz cans corn niblets, drained	*2 × 11½ oz cans corn niblets, drained*
2 × 298 g/10½ oz cans asparagus tips, drained	*2 × 10½ oz cans asparagus tips, drained*
350 g/12 oz Cheddar cheese, grated	*3 cups grated Cheddar cheese*
175 g/6 oz ham, chopped	*¾ cup chopped cooked ham*
8 large spring onions, chopped	*8 large scallions, chopped*
salt	*salt*
freshly ground black pepper	*freshly ground black pepper*
To Garnish:	**To Garnish:**
parsley sprig	*parsley sprig*

Sift the flour and salt into a mixing bowl. Cut and rub in the butter or margarine until the mixture resembles fine breadcrumbs. Bind to a stiff dough with the beaten egg and water. Knead lightly, then divide in half. Roll out on a floured surface and use to line two 25 cm/10 inch flan dishes.

To prepare the filling: Beat the eggs with the cream and milk. Stir in the corn, asparagus, two thirds of the cheese, the ham and spring onions (scallions). Season well with salt and black pepper.

Pour the filling into the flan cases and sprinkle remaining cheese over.

Place in a preheated hot oven (220°C/425°F, Gas Mark 7) and bake for 35 to 40 minutes until golden and set.

Serve hot or cold, garnished with parsley.

STRAWBERRY CHEESECAKE *(page 42)*
(Photograph: Stork Cookery Service)

Pineapple Chicken

METRIC/IMPERIAL
4 × 1.5 kg/3 lb chickens, roasted and
  cooled
4 large pineapples
4 large red peppers, cored, seeded and
  thinly sliced
750 g/1½ lb green grapes, seeded
4 avocados
juice of 1 lemon
300 ml/½ pint mayonnaise (see page
  50)
1½ tablespoons French mustard
300 ml/½ pint soured cream
salt
freshly ground black pepper
To Garnish:
chopped chives

AMERICAN
4 × 3 lb chickens, roasted and cooled
4 large pineapples
4 large red peppers, cored, seeded and
  thinly sliced
6 cups white grapes, pipped
4 avocados
juice of 1 lemon
1¼ cups mayonnaise (see page 50)
1½ tablespoons French mustard
1¼ cups sour cream
salt
freshly ground black pepper
To Garnish:
chopped chives

Remove the meat from the chickens and cut into bite-sized pieces. Place in a large bowl.

Cut the pineapples in half lengthwise right through the leaves. Carefully scoop out the flesh, remove the core and cut the flesh into cubes. Add to the chicken. Reserve the shells for serving.

Add the pepper and grapes to the chicken.

Peel the avocados, cut in half and remove the stone (pit), then cut into 2.5 cm/1 inch pieces. Toss well in the lemon juice to prevent discolouration, then add to the other ingredients.

Combine the mayonnaise, mustard, cream and salt and black pepper to taste and fold into the chicken mixture.

Divide equally between the pineapple shells and sprinkle with chopped chives. Chill before serving.

Chicken Drumsticks en Croûte

METRIC/IMPERIAL
25 chicken drumsticks
350 g/12 oz smooth chicken pâté
salt
freshly ground black pepper
3 × 368 g/13 oz packets frozen puff
  pastry, thawed
3 eggs, beaten
To Garnish:
parsley sprigs

AMERICAN
25 chicken drumsticks
¾ lb smooth chicken pâté
salt
freshly ground black pepper
3 × 13 oz packages frozen puff paste,
  thawed
3 eggs, beaten
To Garnish:
parsley

Spread the drumsticks with pâté and sprinkle with salt and black pepper to taste.

Roll out each packet (package) of pastry (paste) to 5 mm/¼ inch thick and cut into eight 15 cm/6 inch squares. Keep the trimmings and reroll to make the extra square.

Place a drumstick on each piece of pastry (paste), brush the edges with beaten egg and fold over the chicken. Seal the edges well, decorate with any leftover pastry (paste) if liked and brush with beaten egg. Place in a preheated moderately hot oven (200°C/400°F, Gas Mark 6) and bake for 45 minutes until risen and golden.

Serve hot or cold, garnished with parsley.

Tomato Surprises

METRIC/IMPERIAL
25 large tomatoes
500 g/1 lb cottage cheese
2 × 326 g/11½ oz cans sweetcorn,
  drained
salt
freshly ground black pepper

AMERICAN
25 large tomatoes
1 × 1 lb carton ricotta cheese
2 × 11½ oz cans kernel corn, drained
salt
freshly ground black pepper

Cut the stalk ends off the tomatoes and scoop out the centres. Mix the tomato pulp with the cheese, corn, and salt and black pepper to taste. Spoon back into the tomato shells and replace the lids. Chill until required.

Rice Salad

METRIC/IMPERIAL
1 kg/2 lb long-grain rice
150 ml/¼ pint French dressing (see
  below)
225 g/½ lb onions, finely chopped
1 green pepper, cored, seeded and
  finely chopped
1 red pepper, cored, seeded, and
  finely chopped
4 sticks celery, chopped
100 g/4 oz black olives, stoned and
  sliced
2 tablespoons chopped parsley
salt
freshly ground black pepper

AMERICAN
4½ cups long-grain rice
⅔ cup French dressing (see below)
2 cups finely chopped onion
1 green pepper, cored, seeded and
  finely chopped
1 red pepper, cored, seeded and finely
  chopped
4 celery stalks, chopped
¾ cup ripe olives, pitted and sliced
2 tablespoons chopped parsley
salt
freshly ground black pepper

Cook the rice as directed on the packet (package). Drain well and while still hot pour over the dressing and mix thoroughly. Add the remaining ingredients with salt and black pepper to taste.

Turn into two oiled 1.5 litre/2½ pint/5 cup ring moulds and chill for about 2 hours.

Turn out onto 2 plates to serve.

French Dressing

METRIC/IMPERIAL
1½ teaspoons salt
1½ teaspoons dry mustard
1½ teaspoons sugar
1 teaspoon freshly ground black
  pepper
5 tablespoons vinegar
150 ml/¼ pint oil

AMERICAN
1½ teaspoons salt
1½ teaspoons dry mustard
1½ teaspoons sugar
1 teaspoon freshly ground black
  pepper
⅓ cup vinegar
⅔ cup oil

Put all the ingredients in a screw-top jar and shake until thoroughly blended.
Makes about 255 ml/½ pint/1¼ cups

RED FRUIT JELLY (GELATIN) *(page 51)*
(Photograph: Carlsberg)

Mixed Salad

METRIC/IMPERIAL
4 lettuce
2 heads of chicory, sliced
2 bunches of radish, sliced
2 bunches of spring onions, sliced
2 cucumbers, sliced
*2 red peppers, cored, seeded and
 sliced*
mayonnaise to serve (see below)

AMERICAN
4 heads of lettuce
2 heads of Belgian endive, sliced
2 bunches of radish, sliced
2 cucumbers, sliced
2 bunches of scallions, sliced
*2 red peppers, cored, seeded and
 sliced*
mayonnaise to serve (see below)

Place all the prepared ingredients in a large salad bowl and mix well
together. Cover with cling film (saran wrap) and place in the
refrigerator until required. Serve the mayonnaise separately.

Mayonnaise

METRIC/IMPERIAL
6 egg yolks
1 tablespoon dry mustard
1 tablespoon salt
1½ teaspoons white pepper
1 tablespoon sugar
900 ml/1½ pints oil
*6 tablespoons wine vinegar or cider
 vinegar*

AMERICAN
6 egg yolks
1 tablespoon dry mustard
1 tablespoon salt
1½ teaspoons white pepper
1 tablespoon sugar
3¾ cups oil
*6 tablespoons wine vinegar or cider
 vinegar*

Beat the egg yolks in a bowl with the mustard, salt, pepper and sugar.
Using a hand whisk, whisk in the oil drop by drop until the sauce is
thick and smooth. When all the oil has been added, gradually add the
vinegar and mix thoroughly.
Makes 900 ml/1½ pints/3¾ cups

Red Fruit Jelly (Gelatin)

METRIC/IMPERIAL
1.75 kg/4 lb fresh or frozen mixed
  red fruits, e.g. strawberries,
  raspberries, redcurrants
600 ml/1 pint water
100 g/4 oz sugar
4 tablespoons arrowroot
To Serve:
600 ml/1 pint double cream, lightly
  whipped
50–75 g/2–3 oz flaked almonds,
  toasted

AMERICAN
4 lb fresh or frozen mixed red fruits
  e.g. strawberries, raspberries,
  redcurrants
2½ cups water
½ cup sugar
4 tablespoons arrowroot
To Serve:
2½ cups heavy cream, lightly
  whipped
½–¾ cup slivered almonds, toasted

Place the fruit, water and sugar in a pan, bring to the boil, stirring carefully, and simmer gently for about 5 minutes. Work in an electric blender or rub through a coarse sieve until smooth; strain if necessary. Return to the pan.

Blend the arrowroot with a little water and add to fruit, stirring until thickened and smooth. Cool slightly and pour into individual glass serving dishes. Serve with a swirl of cream and a few almonds on each dessert.

Makes 16 to 20

Profiteroles

METRIC/IMPERIAL
Choux Pastry:
600 ml/1 pint milk
225 g/8 oz butter
275 g/10 oz plain flour
large pinch of salt
8 eggs, beaten
Filling:
1.2 litres/2 pints double cream, stiffly
  whipped
Sauce:
1 kg/2 lb plain chocolate
225 g/8 oz unsalted butter
250 ml/8 fl oz milk
120 ml/4 fl oz rum, optional

AMERICAN
Choux Paste:
2½ cups milk
1 cup butter
2½ cups all-purpose flour
large pinch of salt
8 eggs, beaten
Filling:
5 cups heavy cream, stiffly whipped
Sauce:
2 lb semi-sweet chocolate
1 cup sweet butter
1 cup milk
½ cup rum, optional

Put the milk and butter in a saucepan and bring to the boil. Remove from the heat and add the flour and salt, beating well. Add the egg a little at a time, beating well after each addition.

Pipe or spoon the mixture onto greased baking (cookie) sheets to form small buns, leaving plenty of room between them. Bake in batches in a preheated moderately hot oven (200°C/400°F, Gas Mark 6) until well risen and golden brown.

Slit the side of each bun to allow the steam to escape, then place on a wire rack to cool.

To make the chocolate sauce: Place the chocolate, butter and milk together in a bowl over a saucepan of simmering water until mixture is smooth and shiny, stirring occasionally. Remove the bowl from heat and stir in the rum, if using.

When the buns are cold, pipe or spoon whipped cream into the centres through the slits. Place on serving plates to form a pyramid shape. Just before serving, pour hot chocolate sauce over the top.
Makes about 80 buns – allow 3 to 4 per person

PROFITEROLES *(Photographer: Paul Williams)*

DINNER PARTIES

DINNER FOR 2

Curried Macaroni and Ham Salad

Seafood with Leeks
Savoury Rice
Herb Baked Tomatoes

Crêpes à l'Orange

Curried Macaroni and Ham Salad

METRIC/IMPERIAL
40 g/1½ oz short-cut macaroni
salt
75 g/3 oz cooked ham, diced
25 g/1 oz button mushrooms, thinly
  sliced
1 tablespoon wine vinegar
2 teaspoons vegetable oil
white pepper
Dressing:
1½ tablespoons thick mayonnaise
3 tablespoons soured cream
1 teaspoon curry powder
To Garnish:
few black olives
watercress

AMERICAN
⅜ cup elbow macaroni
salt
⅜ cup chopped ham
¼ cup thinly sliced button mushrooms
1 tablespoon wine vinegar
2 teaspoons vegetable oil
white pepper
Dressing:
1¼ tablespoons thick mayonnaise
3 tablespoons sour cream
1 teaspoon curry powder
To Garnish:
few ripe olives
watercress

Cook the macaroni in boiling salted water for 12 to 15 minutes, until *al dente*. Drain, rinse under cold water, and drain well again. Mix with the ham, mushrooms, vinegar, oil, and salt and pepper to taste. Place in a serving dish and chill well.

Mix the dressing ingredients well together.

Just before serving, pour the dressing over the salad and toss well to coat. Garnish with olives and watercress.

Seafood with Leeks

METRIC/IMPERIAL
2 plaice fillets
salt
freshly ground black pepper
5 tablespoons white wine
25 g/1 oz butter
100 g/4 oz leeks, thinly sliced
100 g/4 oz peeled prawns
paprika

AMERICAN
2 flounder fillets
salt
freshly ground black pepper
$\frac{1}{3}$ cup white wine
2 tablespoons butter
$\frac{1}{4}$ lb leeks, thinly sliced
$\frac{2}{3}$ cup shelled shrimp
paprika

Sprinkle the plaice (flounder) with salt and black pepper to taste, fold in half and place in a shallow ovenproof dish. Pour over the wine and cover with foil. Place in a preheated hot oven (200°C/400°F, Gas Mark 6) for 15 to 20 minutes until tender.

Meanwhile, melt the butter in a small pan, add the leeks and sauté until just cooked. Stir in the prawns (shrimp) and season to taste with salt and black pepper.

Place the fish in a serving dish. Pour the cooking liquor into the pan and reheat quickly. Pour over the fish, sprinkle with paprika and serve.

Savoury Rice

METRIC/IMPERIAL
15 g/$\frac{1}{2}$ oz butter
1 rasher streaky bacon, derinded and
* chopped*
1 small onion, chopped
1 small green pepper, cored, seeded
* and chopped*
100 g/4 oz long-grain rice
300 ml/$\frac{1}{2}$ pint chicken stock
salt
freshly ground black pepper

AMERICAN
1 tablespoon butter
1 fatty bacon slice, derinded and
* chopped*
1 small onion, chopped
1 small green pepper, cored, seeded
* and chopped*
$\frac{1}{2}$ cup long-grain rice
1$\frac{1}{4}$ cups chicken bouillon
salt
freshly ground black pepper

Melt the butter in a frying pan (skillet), add the bacon and fry lightly. Add the onion and pepper and fry gently for 5 minutes. Add the rice and cook until transparent, stirring. Pour in the stock (bouillon), add salt and black pepper to taste and bring to the boil. Stir once, then cover and simmer very gently for 15 minutes, until the liquid is absorbed and the rice tender.

Herb Baked Tomatoes

METRIC/IMPERIAL	AMERICAN
4 medium tomatoes, halved	*4 medium tomatoes, halved*
50 g/2 oz butter	*$\frac{1}{4}$ cup butter*
salt	*salt*
freshly ground black pepper	*freshly ground black pepper*
pinch of dried marjoram	*pinch of dried marjoram*

Place the tomatoes in a greased ovenproof dish. Dot with the butter and sprinkle with the salt, black pepper and marjoram. Cover the dish with foil, place in a preheated hot oven (200°C/400°F, Gas Mark 6) and cook for 10 to 15 minutes.

Crêpes à l'orange

METRIC/IMPERIAL	AMERICAN
Pancakes:	**Crêpes:**
50 g/2 oz plain flour	*$\frac{1}{2}$ cup all-purpose flour*
pinch of salt	*pinch of salt*
1 small egg	*1 small egg*
15 g/$\frac{1}{2}$ oz instant dried skimmed milk, plus water to make 150 ml/$\frac{1}{4}$ pint liquid	*1 tablespoon instant dried skimmed milk, plus water to make $\frac{2}{3}$ cup liquid*
oil or lard for frying	*oil or lard for frying*
Orange Sauce:	**Orange Sauce:**
1 orange	*1 orange*
$\frac{1}{2}$ lemon	*$\frac{1}{2}$ lemon*
15 g/$\frac{1}{2}$ oz butter	*1 tablespoon butter*
40 g/1$\frac{1}{2}$ oz caster sugar	*3 tablespoons sugar*
1 tablespoon curaçao	*1 tablespoon curaçao*
1 tablespoon brandy	*1 tablespoon brandy*

Sift the flour and salt into a mixing bowl. Add the egg and gradually beat in half the liquid. Whisk well then leave to stand for at least 1 hour. Stir in remaining liquid just before cooking pancakes (crêpes).

Heat a little oil or lard in a 20 cm/8 inch frying pan (skillet). Pour in just enough batter to cover the base and cook the pancake (crêpe) on both sides until golden brown. Roll up and keep on one side while cooking the remaining batter, making 4 pancakes (crêpes) in all.

Remove zest from the fruit and cut into fine strips. Squeeze out juice.

Melt the butter in a pan and add the fruit juice, sugar, strips of rind and curaçao. Bring to the boil, add the pancakes and allow to heat through slowly. Place the pancakes on a hot serving dish.

Warm the brandy, add to the juice in the pan and ignite. Pour over the pancakes and serve at once.

CREPES A L'ORANGE *(Photograph: The Cadbury Typhoo Food Advisory Service)*

FORMAL DINNER FOR 4

Avocado Proscuitti

Veal with Apples and Port Wine Sauce
Sugar Brown Potatoes
Broccoli

Lemon Syllabub
or
Chocolate Rum Soufflé

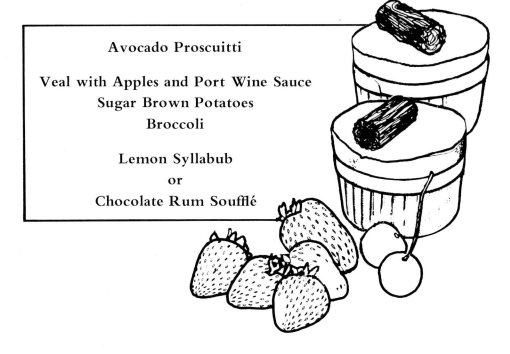

Avocado Proscuitti

METRIC/IMPERIAL
3 oranges
2 avocados
100 g/4 oz Proscuitto ham
To Garnish:
few watercress leaves

AMERICAN
3 oranges
2 avocados
¼ lb Proscuitto ham
To Garnish:
few watercress leaves

Remove the skin and pith from 2 oranges and divide into segments.
Squeeze the juice from the third orange.

Halve the avocados lengthwise, remove the stones (pits) and skin,
then slice the flesh.

Arrange the avocado slices on a large serving dish and sprinkle with
the orange juice.

Cut the ham slices in half, then form into rolls. Arrange decoratively
on the serving dish with the orange segments and garnish with
watercress.

Serve with brown bread.

Veal with Apples and Port

METRIC/IMPERIAL
4 veal escalopes or cutlets
15 g/½ oz plain flour
75 g/3 oz butter
salt
freshly ground black pepper
4 tablespoons port or Madeira wine
150 ml/¼ pint chicken stock
  (approximately)
2–3 dessert apples, cored and sliced
1 × 142 ml/5 fl oz carton double
  cream
25 g/1 oz flaked almonds
2 tablespoons lemon juice

AMERICAN
4 veal escalopes or cutlets
2 tablespoons all-purpose flour
⅓ cup butter
salt
freshly ground black pepper
4 tablespoons port or Madeira wine
⅔ cup chicken bouillon
  (approximately)
2–3 dessert apples, cored and sliced
⅔ cup heavy cream
¼ cup blanched slivered almonds
2 tablespoons lemon juice

Trim the escalopes neatly and coat with flour. Melt half the butter in a frying pan (skillet) and fry the escalopes until golden brown on both sides. Add salt and black pepper to taste, then the port or Madeira. Simmer, uncovered, until slightly reduced.

Add enough stock (bouillon) just to cover the meat, cover and simmer gently until meat is tender, 20 to 40 minutes, depending on thickness.

Meanwhile, melt the remaining butter in a clean pan, add the apple slices and fry until golden.

Place the escalopes on a warm serving dish, garnish with the apple slices and keep warm.

Mix a little of the sauce into the cream, return to the pan and cook gently until thickened. Add the almonds, check the seasoning and pour over the meat. Sprinkle the apples with lemon juice and serve immediately.

Sugar Brown Potatoes

METRIC/IMPERIAL	AMERICAN
500 g/1 lb small new potatoes	1 lb small new potatoes
salt	salt
50 g/2 oz caster sugar	$\frac{1}{4}$ cup sugar
50 g/2 oz butter	$\frac{1}{4}$ cup butter

Cook the potatoes in boiling, salted water until just tender. Drain and keep warm.

Place the sugar in a heavy-based pan and heat very slowly, stirring constantly, until the sugar has melted and is light brown in colour.

Stir in the butter. When it has melted, add the potatoes and toss carefully until they are evenly coated.

Lemon Syllabub

METRIC/IMPERIAL	AMERICAN
grated rind and juice of 1 lemon	grated rind and juice of 1 lemon
100 g/4 oz caster sugar	$\frac{1}{2}$ cup superfine sugar
150 ml/$\frac{1}{4}$ pint sweet white wine or sherry	$\frac{2}{3}$ cup sweet white wine or sherry
1 × 284 ml/10 fl oz carton double cream	$1\frac{1}{4}$ cups heavy cream
sponge fingers to serve	lady fingers to serve

Mix together the lemon rind and juice, sugar and wine or sherry and leave to stand for at least 1 hour. Strain into a mixing bowl, then add the cream. Whisk until the mixture thickens. Spoon into tall glasses and chill well. Serve with sponge fingers (lady fingers).

CHOCOLATE RUM SOUFFLE *(page 62)*
(Photograph: Brown & Polson)

Chocolate Rum Soufflé

METRIC/IMPERIAL

25 g/1 oz cornflour
3 eggs, separated
100 g/4 oz caster sugar
450 ml/¾ pint milk
100 g/4 oz plain chocolate, broken
  up
15 g/½ oz gelatine
3 tablespoons warm water
1½ tablespoons rum

To Decorate:

chopped nuts
1 × 142 ml/5 fl oz carton double
  cream, whipped
chocolate triangles (see below)

AMERICAN

¼ cup cornstarch
3 eggs, separated
½ cup superfine sugar
2 cups milk
4 squares semi-sweet chocolate,
  broken up
2 envelopes gelatin
3 tablespoons water
1½ tablespoons rum

To Decorate:

chopped nuts
⅔ cup heavy cream, whipped
chocolate triangles (see below)

Tie a double band of oiled foil or greaseproof (waxed) paper around a 13 cm/5 inch soufflé dish so that the band stands about 7.5 cm/3 inches above the rim.

Blend the cornflour (cornstarch), egg yolks and sugar with a little of the milk to make a smooth cream. Put the remaining milk in a pan and heat to just below boiling point. Pour onto the cornflour (cornstarch), mix well, then return to the pan and bring to the boil, stirring. Simmer for 3 minutes, stirring continuously. Remove from the heat, add the chocolate and stir until melted.

Place the gelatine and warm water in a bowl over a pan of simmering water and stir until dissolved. Add to the pan with the rum and cool slightly.

Whisk the egg whites stiffly, fold into the mixture, then pour into the prepared soufflé dish. Place in the refrigerator until set.

Remove the paper carefully and coat the sides of the soufflé with chopped nuts. Decorate the top with swirls of cream and chocolate triangles.

To make chocolate triangles: Melt 50 g/2 oz/2 squares plain (semi-sweet) chocolate in a bowl over a pan of hot water. Pour onto a flat piece of foil or non-stick paper and spread out thinly. Leave to cool slightly, mark into squares, then into triangles. Leave to set then cut into triangles and peel off the foil or paper.

INFORMAL DINNER FOR 6

Fish and Bacon Chowder

Polynesian Roast Chicken
Roast Potatoes
Glazed Carrots   Courgettes

Apple Cheesecake

Fish and Bacon Chowder

METRIC/IMPERIAL
75 g/3 oz butter
1 large onion, thinly sliced
175 g/6 oz back bacon, derinded and
  cut into strips
6 sticks celery, sliced
1 green pepper, cored, seeded and
  chopped
2 medium potatoes, diced
450 ml/$\frac{3}{4}$ pint fish or chicken stock
500 g/1 lb white fish (huss, cod,
  whiting), skinned, boned and cut
  into small pieces
1$\frac{1}{2}$ tablespoons cornflour, blended
  with 600 ml/1 pint milk
175 g/6 oz mussels
4 tomatoes, skinned and chopped
6 tablespoons double cream
salt
freshly ground black pepper
To Garnish:
chopped parsley

AMERICAN
$\frac{1}{3}$ cup butter
1 large onion, thinly sliced
$\frac{3}{4}$ cup chopped Canadian bacon slices
6 celery stalks, sliced
1 green pepper, cored, seeded and
  chopped
2 medium potatoes, diced
2 cups fish or chicken bouillon
1 lb white fish (hake, cod, whiting),
  skinned, boned, and cut into small
  pieces
1$\frac{1}{2}$ tablespoons cornstarch, blended
  with 2$\frac{1}{2}$ cups milk
6 oz mussels
4 tomatoes, skinned and chopped
6 tablespoons heavy cream
salt
freshly ground black pepper
To Garnish:
chopped parsley

Melt the butter in a large pan and gently cook the onion, bacon, celery,
pepper and potatoes for 5 to 8 minutes, until soft but not brown. Add
the stock (bouillon) and cook until the potatoes are almost done.

Add the fish to the pan, then stir in the blended cornflour
(cornstarch). Bring slowly to the boil, stirring occasionally, then simmer
very gently for about 5 minutes.

Add the mussels, tomatoes and cream and reheat gently. Season
carefully with salt and plenty of black pepper and sprinkle with parsley.
Serve very hot with crusty bread.

Polynesian Roast Chicken

METRIC/IMPERIAL
1 × 2 kg/4½ lb oven-ready chicken
3 tablespoons cooking oil
1 × 822 g/1 lb 13 oz can pineapple
  rings
To Garnish:
watercress
Sauce:
1½ tablespoons salad oil
6 tablespoons peanut butter
200 ml/⅓ pint tomato ketchup
4 tablespoons Worcestershire sauce
garlic powder
salt

AMERICAN
1 × 4½ lb oven ready chicken
3 tablespoons cooking oil
1 × 2 lb can pineapple rings
To Garnish:
watercress
Sauce:
1½ tablespoons salad oil
6 tablespoons peanut butter
⅞ cup tomato catsup
¼ cup Worcestershire sauce
garlic powder
salt

First prepare the sauce. Heat the salad oil gently in a pan, then add the peanut butter. Continue heating, stirring occasionally, until the peanut butter begins to thicken and change colour. Remove from the heat immediately and stir in the ketchup (catsup) and Worcestershire sauce. Add garlic powder and salt to taste. Leave for 2 hours before using.

Place the chicken in a roasting pan and spoon over the cooking oil. Roast in a preheated moderately hot oven (200°C/400°F, Gas Mark 6) for 1 hour, basting occasionally. Brush 2 tablespoons of the peanut sauce over the chicken and return to the oven for 10 minutes until a rich brown colour.

Drain the pineapple; reserving 3 tablespoons of the juice. Arrange the pineapple on an ovenproof serving dish and warm gently in the oven. Place the chicken on top and garnish with watercress.

Blend the reserved pineapple juice into the peanut sauce and reheat gently. Serve the sauce separately.

FISH AND BACON CHOWDER (page 63)
(Photograph: The White Fish Kitchen)

Glazed Carrots

METRIC/IMPERIAL	AMERICAN
75 g/3 oz butter	⅓ cup butter
750 g/1½ lb young carrots, scraped and left whole	1½ lb young carrots, scraped and left whole
4 lumps of sugar	4 lumps of sugar
½ teaspoon salt	½ teaspoon salt
a little chicken stock	a little chicken bouillon
To Garnish:	**To Garnish:**
chopped parsley	chopped parsley

Melt the butter in a saucepan. Add the carrots, sugar, salt and enough stock (bouillon) to half cover the carrots. Cook very gently, without a lid, until tender, shaking the pan occasionally. Remove the carrots from the pan, place in a serving dish and keep warm.

Boil the liquid in the pan to reduce to a rich glaze. Pour over the carrots, toss well to coat, and sprinkle with parsley.

Apple Cheesecake

METRIC/IMPERIAL	AMERICAN
100 g/4 oz shortcrust pastry, made with 100 g/4 oz plain flour	1 cup basic pie dough, made with 1 cup all-purpose flour
6 tablespoons Guinness	6 tablespoons Guinness
100 g/4 oz currants	¾ cup currants
500 g/1 lb cream cheese, sieved	1 × 1 lb carton cream cheese, sieved
2 eggs, beaten	2 eggs, beaten
2 tablespoons cornflour	2 tablespoons cornstarch
grated rind of 1 lemon	grated rind of 1 lemon
1–2 red dessert apples, cored, quartered and thinly sliced	1–2 red dessert apples, cored, quartered and thinly sliced
sieved apricot jam	sieved apricot jam

Roll out the prepared pastry (paste) and use to line a 20 cm/8 inch round sandwich tin (layercake pan) or flan ring.

Put the Guinness and currants in a saucepan and bring to the boil. Remove from the heat and leave to cool.

Beat the cheese and eggs well together, sprinkle the cornflour (cornstarch) and lemon rind on top and mix well in. Stir in the Guinness and currants and pour into the flan case. Place in a preheated moderate oven (180°C/350°F, Gas Mark 4) and bake for 1 hour. Leave in the tin to cool. Place the flan on a serving dish, arrange the apple slices on top and brush with apricot jam. Serve with pouring cream.

FORMAL DINNER FOR 6

Grapefruit Cups

Harvest Crown of Lamb
Anna Potatoes
Baby Brussels Sprouts

Mandarin Pavlovas
or
Strawberry Ice Cream

Grapefruit Cups

METRIC/IMPERIAL

3 grapefruit
1 red dessert apple, cored and
  chopped
7.5 cm/3 inch piece of cucumber, cut
  into 1 cm/$\frac{1}{2}$ inch cubes
3 sticks celery, cut into 1 cm/$\frac{1}{2}$ inch
  cubes
12 black olives or grapes, seeded and
  halved
3 tablespoons clear honey
3 tablespoons wine vinegar
$\frac{1}{2}$ teaspoon French mustard
To Garnish:
1$\frac{1}{2}$ tablespoons chopped mint or
  parsley

AMERICAN

3 grapefruit
1 red dessert apple, cored and
  chopped
3 inch piece of cucumber, cut into $\frac{1}{2}$
  inch cubes
3 celery stalks, cut into $\frac{1}{2}$ inch cubes
12 ripe olives or purple grapes,
  pipped and halved
3 tablespoons clear honey
3 tablespoons wine vinegar
$\frac{1}{2}$ teaspoon French mustard
To Garnish:
1$\frac{1}{2}$ tablespoons chopped mint or
  parsley

Cut the grapefruit in half and remove the segments, discarding any pith
and membrane. Reserve the shells.

Mix together the grapefruit, apple, cucumber, celery and olives or
grapes.

Blend the remaining ingredients together and pour over the fruit.
Toss together well to coat and chill until required.

Serve in the grapefruit shells, garnished with the mint or parsley.

Harvest Crown of Lamb

METRIC/IMPERIAL
2 best ends of neck of lamb (12
  cutlets)
1 tablespoon oil
1 small onion, chopped
1 stick celery, chopped
100 g/4 oz carrots, chopped
25 g/1 oz sultanas
500 g/1 lb cooking apples, peeled and
  diced
50 g/2 oz long-grain rice, cooked
2 tablespoons chopped parsley
salt
freshly ground black pepper
lemon juice to taste
450 ml/¾ pint dry cider or apple juice
1 tablespoon cornflour, blended with
  2 tablespoons water
To Garnish:
2 red dessert apples, cored and cut
  into wedges
watercress
12 cutlet frills

AMERICAN
2 racks of lamb (12 ribs)
1 tablespoon oil
1 small onion, chopped
1 celery stalk, chopped
¾ cup chopped carrots
3 tablespoons seedless white raisins
4 cups peeled and diced baking
  apples
¼ cup long-grain rice, cooked
2 tablespoons chopped parsley
salt
freshly ground black pepper
lemon juice to taste
2 cups hard cider or apple juice
1 tablespoon cornstarch blended with
  2 tablespoons water
To Garnish:
2 red dessert apples, cored and cut
  into wedges
watercress
12 rib frills

Ask the butcher to prepare the lamb and form it into a crown; keep the trimmings.

Heat the oil in a frying pan (skillet), add the onion and celery and fry gently until soft. Add the carrots, sultanas (seedless white raisins) and apples and continue cooking, stirring occasionally, for a few minutes. Add the rice and parsley and season well with salt, black pepper and lemon juice.

Stand the crown in a greased roasting pan and fill with the stuffing, pressing it down well. Cover with some of the fat trimmings. Cover the ends of the cutlet (rib) bones with foil to prevent them burning. Brush the outside of the crown lightly with oil, place in a preheated moderately hot oven (190°C/375°F, Gas Mark 5) and cook for 1¼ to 2 hours, depending on size, until tender. Place the crown on a hot serving dish.

Carefully pour off the fat from the roasting pan, leaving the juices. Add the cider or apple juice to the pan, scraping up the sediment from the bottom of the pan. Add the blended cornflour (cornstarch) and salt and black pepper to taste. Bring to the boil, stirring, and cook until thickened. Pour into a gravy boat.

Remove the foil and string from the crown and place a paper frill on the end of each cutlet (rib). Garnish with apple and watercress.

GRAPEFRUIT CUPS (page 67) (Photograph: Fyffes Group)

Anna Potatoes

METRIC/IMPERIAL
1.25 kg/2½ lb potatoes, thinly sliced
salt
freshly ground black pepper
100 g/4 oz butter, melted

AMERICAN
2½ lb potatoes, thinly sliced
salt
freshly ground black pepper
½ cup butter, melted

Grease and base-line a 20–23 cm/8–9 inch round cake tin (pan) and arrange a layer of slightly overlapping potato slices on the bottom. Sprinkle with salt and black pepper and pour over a little melted butter.

Continue the layers in this way until all the potatoes have been used, pressing each layer well down into the tin (pan).

Cover with greaseproof (waxed) paper and a lid or foil and bake in a preheated moderately hot oven (190°C/375°F, Gas Mark 5) for 1¼ hours, adding more butter if the potatoes begin to look dry. Turn out and serve at once.

Strawberry Ice Cream

METRIC/IMPERIAL
2 eggs
75 g/3 oz caster sugar
300 ml/½ pint milk
300 ml/½ pint unsweetened thick
  strawberry purée
1 × 284 ml/10 fl oz carton double
  cream, lightly whipped

AMERICAN
2 eggs
⅓ cup superfine sugar
1¼ cups milk
1¼ cups unsweetened thick strawberry
  paste
1¼ cups heavy cream, lightly
  whipped

Whisk the eggs and sugar together.

Heat the milk to just below boiling point, then whisk into the eggs and sugar to form a custard. Return to the heat and cook, stirring until thickened; do *not* let the custard boil. Strain into a bowl and cover with cling film (saran wrap) to prevent a skin forming. Leave to cool.

Fold in the strawberry purée (paste) and cream. Pour into a plastic container and freeze for about 30 minutes, then turn into a bowl and whisk thoroughly. Pour into a carton and freeze.

To serve, place the ice cream in the refrigerator for about 1 hour to soften slightly. Scoop into individual glass dishes and serve with ice cream wafers.

Mandarin Pavlovas

METRIC/IMPERIAL	AMERICAN
3 egg whites	*3 egg whites*
175 g/6 oz caster sugar	*¾ cup superfine sugar*
2 teaspoons cornflour	*2 teaspoons cornstarch*
1 teaspoon lemon juice	*1 teaspoon lemon juice*
½ teaspoon vanilla essence	*½ teaspoon vanilla extract*
1 × 142 ml/5 fl oz carton double cream, stiffly whipped	*⅔ cup heavy cream, stiffly whipped*
1 × 454 g/1 lb can mandarin oranges, drained	*1 × 1 lb can mandarin oranges, drained*
To Decorate:	**To Decorate:**
glacé cherries and angelica (optional)	*candied cherries and angelica (optional)*

Whisk the egg whites until stiff, then whisk in half the sugar, a little at a time. Fold in the remaining sugar, then fold in the cornflour (cornstarch), lemon juice and vanilla essence (extract).

Cover 3 large baking (cookie) sheets with non-stick paper and mark four 7.5 cm/3 inch rounds on each.

Place the meringue in a piping (pastry) bag fitted with a large plain or star nozzle and pipe the mixture onto the prepared circles, starting from the centre.

Place in a preheated cool oven (140°C/275°F, Gas Mark 1) for 30 minutes, then lower the heat to 120°C/250°F, Gas Mark ½ and leave in the oven for a further 30 to 40 minutes until crisp and dry. Change over the top and bottom baking (cookie) sheets halfway through cooking.

Cool slightly, then carefully remove the paper. Place the meringues carefully on wire racks and leave until completely cold.

Place one meringue round on an individual serving plate. Cover with piped cream and top with mandarins. Place another meringue ring on top. Repeat with the remaining meringues.

Decorate the tops with any remaining cream and fruit, and add cherries and angelica if liked.

FORMAL DINNER FOR 8

Crab and Lettuce Mousse

Lamb en Croûte
Duchess Potatoes
Glazed Carrots   Broad Beans

Raspberry Cheesecake
or
Apricot Chiffon

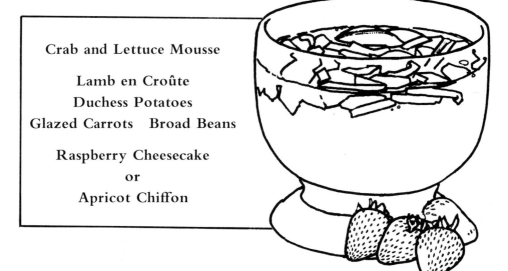

Crab and Lettuce Mousse

METRIC/IMPERIAL
350 g/12 oz canned or frozen crab
  meat
2 teaspoons powdered gelatine
5 tablespoons fish stock
juice of 1 lemon
grated rind of $\frac{1}{2}$ lemon
salt
freshly ground black pepper
pinch of cayenne pepper
1 lettuce, very finely shredded
200 ml/$\frac{1}{3}$ pint double cream, lightly
  whipped
To Garnish:
cucumber slices
lemon wedges
parsley sprigs

AMERICAN
$\frac{3}{4}$ lb canned or frozen crab meat
2 teaspoons powdered gelatin
$\frac{1}{3}$ cup fish bouillon
juice of 1 lemon
grated rind of $\frac{1}{2}$ lemon
salt
freshly ground black pepper
pinch of cayenne pepper
1 head of lettuce, very finely
  shredded
$\frac{7}{8}$ cup heavy cream, lightly whipped
To Garnish:
cucumber slices
lemon wedges
parsley sprigs

Beat the crab meat until smooth. Place the gelatine (gelatin) and stock (bouillon) in a basin over a pan of hot water and stir until the gelatine (gelatin) is dissolved. Add to the crab with the lemon juice and rind, salt and black pepper to taste, cayenne and shredded lettuce. Fold in the cream. Cover and leave in the refrigerator until required.

Spoon the mousse into individual dishes and garnish with cucumber, lemon and parsley. Serve with thinly sliced brown bread and butter.

LAMB EN CROUTE (page 74) (Photograph: The New Zealand
Lamb Information Bureau)

Lamb en Croûte

METRIC/IMPERIAL	AMERICAN
1.75 kg/4 lb leg of lamb, boned	4 lb leg of lamb, boned
dried rosemary	dried rosemary
dried sage	dried sage
salt	salt
freshly ground black pepper	freshly ground black pepper
1 × 378 g/13 oz packet frozen puff pastry, thawed	1 × 13 oz package frozen puff paste, thawed
1 egg, beaten	1 egg, beaten

Sprinkle the lamb with rosemary, sage, salt and black pepper to taste. Place in a roasting pan and cook in a preheated moderate oven (180°C/350°F, Gas Mark 4) for about $1\frac{1}{2}$ hours, until almost cooked. Leave to cool. Increase the oven temperature to 220°C/425°F, Gas Mark 7.

Roll out the pastry (paste) to a rectangle 50 × 25 cm/20 × 10 inches. Brush the edges with beaten egg. Place the lamb in the centre of the pastry (paste) and fold it over to enclose the lamb completely and make a neat parcel. Trim and seal the edges well together. Decorate with rounds cut from the trimmings and brush with beaten egg.

Return to the oven and cook for 30 minutes until golden brown.

Duchess Potatoes

METRIC/IMPERIAL	AMERICAN
1.75 kg/4 lb potatoes, cooked and mashed	4 lb potatoes, cooked and mashed
50 g/2 oz butter	$\frac{1}{4}$ cup butter
1 large egg	1 large egg
1 teaspoon salt	1 teaspoon salt
freshly ground black pepper	freshly ground black pepper
pinch of grated nutmeg	pinch of grated nutmeg

Beat all the ingredients well together. Grease a baking (cookie) sheet.

Using a piping (pastry) bag with a large star nozzle, pipe the potato into 16 pyramid shapes, each with a base of about 5 cm/2 inches. Brush each with a little melted butter. Place in a preheated hot oven (220°C/425°F, Gas Mark 7) and cook for about 15 to 20 minutes until lightly browned.

Raspberry Cheesecake

METRIC/IMPERIAL

Base:
100 g/4 oz digestive biscuits, crushed
25 g/1 oz demerara sugar
50 g/2 oz butter, melted

Filling:
15 g/½ oz gelatine
2 tablespoons hot water
175 g/6 oz soft cream cheese
juice and finely grated rind of 1
  lemon
2 eggs, separated
50 g/2 oz caster sugar
4 tablespoons double cream

To Decorate:
225 g/8 oz raspberries
150 ml/¼ pint double cream, whipped

AMERICAN

Base:
1½ cups Graham cracker crumbs
¼ cup brown sugar
¼ cup butter, melted

Filling:
¾ cup soft cream cheese
2 envelopes gelatin
2 tablespoons hot water
¾ cup soft cream cheese
juice and finely grated rind of 1
  lemon
2 eggs, separated
¼ cup superfine sugar
¼ cup heavy cream

To Decorate:
1½ cups raspberries
⅔ cup heavy cream, whipped

Mix all the ingredients for the base together. Press into a well greased 20 cm/8 inch loose bottomed cake tin (pan) and place in the refrigerator until firm.

Place the gelatine (gelatin) and hot water in a basin over a pan of simmering water and add to the cheese, blending well. Whisk together the lemon juice and rind, egg yolks and sugar then beat in the cream and cheese.

Whisk the egg whites until stiff and then gently fold into cheese mixture. Pour over the base and return to the refrigerator for at least 2 hours to set.

Just before serving, remove the cheesecake from the tin (pan) and decorate with raspberries and cream.

Serves 8

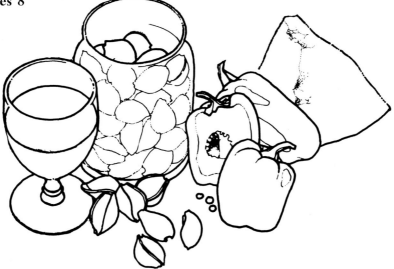

Apricot Chiffon

METRIC/IMPERIAL
2 × 425 g/15 oz cans apricot halves
100 g/4 oz cornflour
175 g/6 oz sugar
4 eggs, separated
1.2 litres/2 pints milk
2 teaspoons lemon juice
3–4 drops almond essence
To Decorate:
whipped cream
toasted flaked almonds

AMERICAN
2 × 15 oz cans apricot halves
1 cup cornstarch
$\frac{3}{4}$ cup sugar, firmly packed
4 eggs, separated
5 cups milk
2 teaspoons lemon juice
3–4 drops almond extract
To Decorate:
whipped cream
toasted flaked almonds

Reserve 8 apricot halves for decoration and liquidize or sieve (strain) the remainder with the juice.

Blend the cornflour (cornstarch), 100 g/4 oz/$\frac{1}{2}$ cup of the sugar and the egg yolks with a little of the milk. Put the remaining milk in a pan and heat gently, then add to the cornflour (cornstarch). Return to the pan and bring to the boil, then simmer for 3 minutes, stirring constantly.

Remove from the heat and add the sieved (strained) apricots, lemon juice and almond essence (extract).

Whisk the egg whites until stiff, fold in the remaining sugar, then fold gently into the apricot mixture.

Spoon into 8 individual dishes or glasses and leave to chill in the refrigerator. Decorate with rosettes of cream, flaked almonds and the reserved apricot halves. Serve chilled.
Serves 8

RASPBERRY CHEESECAKE *(page 75) (Photograph: Eden Vale)*

CHILDREN'S PARTY

Sandwich Selection
Sausages on Potato Sticks
Cheese and Pineapple on Potato Sticks
Crisps, potato rings, etc.

Trifle or Chocolate and Pear Mice
Viennese Fingers
Shortbread Animals
Oaty Crunchies
Honey Raisin Bars
Country Teapot Cake or Clock Cake

Oaty Crunchies

METRIC/IMPERIAL	AMERICAN
75 g/3 oz plain flour	$\frac{3}{4}$ cup all-purpose flour
75 g/3 oz caster sugar	$\frac{3}{8}$ cup sugar
75 g/3 oz rolled oats	1 cup rolled oats
75 g/3 oz butter	$\frac{1}{3}$ cup butter
1 tablespoon golden syrup	1 tablespoon maple syrup
1 tablespoon milk	1 tablespoon milk
$\frac{1}{2}$ teaspoon bicarbonate of soda	$\frac{1}{2}$ teaspoon baking soda

Mix the flour, sugar and oats together in a bowl. Place the butter, syrup and milk in a pan and heat gently until melted. Stir in the bicarbonate of soda (baking soda) then pour onto the dry ingredients.

Shape the mixture into 20 balls and place well apart on two greased baking (cookie) sheets. Bake in a preheated cool oven (150°C/300°F, Gas Mark 2) for 20 minutes. Leave to cool slightly for 3 minutes then transfer to a wire rack.
Makes 20

Country Teapot Cake

METRIC/IMPERIAL	AMERICAN
250 g/8 oz self-raising flour	2 cups self-rising flour
1½ teaspoons baking powder	1½ teaspoons baking powder
175 g/6 oz soft margarine	¾ cup soft margarine
175 g/6 oz caster sugar	¾ cup superfine sugar
3 eggs	3 eggs
250 g/8 oz glacé cherries, halved	1 cup candied cherries, halved
50 g/2 oz ground almonds	½ cup ground almonds
Filling:	**Filling:**
3 tablespoons raspberry jam	3 tablespoons raspberry preserves
To Decorate:	**To Decorate:**
300 g/10 oz prepared almond paste	10 oz almond paste
few drops of orange and green food colouring	few drops of orange and green food coloring
4 tablespoons apricot jam, sieved	4 tablespoons apricot preserves, sieved
hundreds and thousands	sugar strands
1 tablespoon chocolate glacé icing	1 tablespoon chocolate glacé icing

Sift the flour and baking powder into a bowl, add the remaining cake ingredients and beat with a wooden spoon until well mixed, 2 to 3 minutes. Place in a greased 1.2 litre/2 pint/5 cup pudding basin (ovenproof bowl) and bake in the centre of a preheated moderate oven (160°C/325°F, Gas Mark 3) for 1 to 1¼ hours until firm to the touch. Cool on a wire rack.

Cut the cake horizontally in three and sandwich together with the raspberry jam (preserves).

Reserve a small piece of the almond paste. Colour the rest orange and roll out half of it thinly on a sugared surface. Brush the cake with the apricot jam (preserves) and cover with the paste. Stand the cake on a cake board.

Using the remaining orange paste, shape a spout and handle for the teapot. Cut out a circle for a lid, using a pastry (cookie) cutter, roll a small ball in the hands and fix to the centre of the 'lid' with apricot jam (preserves). Attach the handle, spout and lid to the cake with a little apricot jam (preserves); they may need supporting until dry.

Colour a small piece of almond paste green, cut into an oblong and position for a door. From the remaining white paste, cut out 4 windows; make doorsteps and a porch if liked.

Brush the top half of 'windows' with apricot jam (preserves) and sprinkle over a few hundreds and thousands (sugar strands) to represent curtains. Fix door, windows (and porch and steps if made), to the cake with apricot jam. Put the chocolate icing in a piping (pastry) bag fitted with fine nozzle and pipe 2 lines on the windows to represent panes and a handle on the door.

Chocolate and Pear Mice

METRIC/IMPERIAL
50 g/2 oz butter
2 tablespoons golden syrup
1 tablespoon cocoa powder
65 g/2½ oz rice crispies
1 packet chocolate blancmange
  powder
600 ml/1 pint milk
1 × 411 g/14½ oz can pear halves,
  drained
To Decorate:
almond flakes
currants
glacé cherries
angelica

AMERICAN
¼ cup butter
2 tablespoons maple syrup
1 tablespoon unsweetened cocoa
2½ cups rice crispies
1 package chocolate blancmange
  powder
1 pint milk
1 × 14½ oz can pear halves, drained
To Decorate:
almond flakes
currants
candied cherries
angelica

Place the butter and syrup in a pan and heat gently until melted. Stir in the cocoa and rice crispies.

Press the mixture into a 20 cm/7 inch flan ring or pie plate, and place in the refrigerator to set. Then make up the blancmange as directed on the packet and pour over the set chocolate base. Return to the refrigerator to set the blancmange.

Place the pear halves on the blancmange and decorate with almond flake ears, currant eyes, cherry noses and angelica tails.
Serves 6

Honey Raisin Bars

METRIC/IMPERIAL
75 g/3 oz butter
175 g/6 oz clear honey
3 eggs, beaten
175 g/6 oz plain flour
1 teaspoon baking powder
175 g/6 oz raisins
100 g/4 oz walnuts, chopped

AMERICAN
⅓ cup butter
½ cup clear honey
3 eggs, beaten
1½ cups all-purpose flour
1 teaspoon baking powder
1 cup raisins
1 cup chopped walnuts

Beat the butter and honey together until soft, then beat in the eggs. Sift the flour and baking powder together, then gradually fold into the butter mixture, with the raisins and walnuts.

Press onto a well-greased Swiss roll tin (jelly roll pan) and bake in a preheated moderate oven (180°C/350°F, Gas Mark 4) for 30 minutes, or until golden brown and firm to touch. Cool slightly, then cut into bars.
Makes about 18

CHOCOLATE AND PEAR MICE (Photograph: Brown & Polson)

Viennese Fingers

METRIC/IMPERIAL	AMERICAN
250 g/8 oz butter	1 cup butter
50 g/2 oz caster sugar	$\frac{1}{4}$ cup sugar
$\frac{1}{4}$ teaspoon vanilla essence	$\frac{1}{4}$ teaspoon vanilla extract
250 g/8 oz plain flour, sifted	2 cups all-purpose flour, sifted
pinch of salt	pinch of salt
To Decorate:	**To Decorate:**
50 g/2 oz chocolate, melted	2 squares chocolate, melted

Cream the butter and sugar together until fluffy. Beat in the vanilla essence (extract), then gradually beat in the flour and salt. Spoon the mixture into a piping (pastry) bag fitted with a large star nozzle and pipe in 7.5 cm/3 inch lengths, spaced well apart, on well-greased baking (cookie) sheets. Place in a preheated moderately hot oven (190°C/375°F, Gas Mark 5) and bake for 15 to 20 minutes, or until lightly browned and crisp. Cool on a wire rack. Just before serving, dip the ends of the fingers into melted chocolate.

Makes about 36

Shortbread Animals

METRIC/IMPERIAL	AMERICAN
175 g/6 oz plain flour	$1\frac{1}{2}$ cups all-purpose flour
pinch of salt	pinch of salt
100 g/4 oz margarine	$\frac{1}{2}$ cup margarine
50 g/2 oz caster sugar	$\frac{1}{4}$ cup sugar
Icing:	**Icing:**
100 g/4 oz icing sugar, sifted	1 cup confectioners' sugar, sifted
1–2 teaspoons water	1–2 teaspoons water
To Decorate:	**To Decorate:**
sweets, chocolate vermicelli	sweets, chocolate vermicelli

Sift the flour and salt together, then cut and rub in the margarine until the mixture resembles breadcrumbs. Stir in the sugar, then knead lightly to bind together.

Turn onto a floured board and roll out to 1 cm/$\frac{1}{2}$ inch thickness. Cut into 20 to 24 biscuits using different animal cutters and place on greased baking (cookie) sheets.

Place in a preheated moderate oven (160°C/325°F, Gas Mark 3) and bake for 20 to 30 minutes until golden. Cool on a wire rack.

Mix the icing sugar with enough water to make a coating consistency and spoon onto the biscuits. Decorate as liked, with sweets or chocolate vermicelli.

Makes 20 to 24

Trifle

METRIC/IMPERIAL

1 pineapple jelly
3 bananas
1 chocolate Swiss roll
2 tablespoons cocoa powder
1 tablespoon cornflour
2 tablespoons sugar
600 ml/1 pint milk
1 × 142 ml/5 fl oz carton double
  cream, lightly whipped
little lemon juice
4 glacé cherries, halved

AMERICAN

1 package of pineapple-flavored
  gelatin
3 bananas
1 chocolate jelly roll
2 tablespoons unsweetened cocoa
1 tablespoon cornstarch
2 tablespoons sugar
1 pint milk
⅔ cup heavy cream, lightly whipped
little lemon juice
4 candied cherries

Make up the jelly (flavored gelatin) following the packet (package) instructions. When on the point of setting, slice 2 bananas and stir them into the jelly. Pour into a glass dish.

Cut the Swiss roll (jelly roll) into 8 slices and arrange upright around the edge so that the ends set in the jelly.

Blend the cocoa, cornflour (cornstarch) and sugar with a little of the milk. Put the remaining milk in a pan and heat to just below boiling point, then pour it onto the cocoa mixture. Return the custard to the pan, bring to the boil, and boil for 2 minutes, stirring constantly. Leave to cool.

Fold the cream into the cold custard and pour onto the jelly.

Just before serving, decorate the trifle with the remaining banana, sliced and dipped in lemon juice, and cherries.
Serves 8

Clock Cake

<table>
<tr><td>

METRIC/IMPERIAL
100 g/4 oz butter
100 g/4 oz caster sugar
2 eggs, beaten
100 g/4 oz self-raising flour
grated rind of 1 orange
Filling:
2 tablespoons orange juice
25 g/1 oz caster sugar
1 × 142 ml/5 fl oz carton double cream
To Decorate:
50 g/2 oz icing sugar
25 g/1 oz cocoa powder
2–3 teaspoons water
25 small sweets

</td><td>

AMERICAN
½ cup butter
½ cup sugar
2 eggs, beaten
1 cup self-rising flour
grated rind of 1 orange
Filling:
2 tablespoons orange juice
2 tablespoons sugar
⅔ cup heavy cream
To Decorate:
½ cup confectioners' sugar
¼ cup unsweetened cocoa
2–3 teaspoons water
25 small sweets

</td></tr>
</table>

Brush two 18 cm/7 inch sandwich tins (layer cake pans) with melted butter, then dust lightly with flour.

Cream together the butter and sugar until light and fluffy, then gradually beat in the eggs. Lightly fold in the flour, using a metal spoon, then stir in the orange rind.

Transfer the mixture to the prepared tins (pans) and smooth the tops. Bake in the centre of a preheated moderate oven (180°C/350°F, Gas Mark 4) for 25 to 30 minutes until golden brown and firm to the touch. Turn out onto a wire rack to cool.

To make the filling: Add the orange juice and the sugar to the cream and whip together until stiff. Use some of the cream to sandwich the sponges together and spread the rest over the top.

Sift the icing (confectioners') sugar and cocoa together into a small bowl, add the water and mix until smooth. Place in a piping (pastry) bag fitted with a large star nozzle and pipe a border around the outside edge of the cake.

Arrange 24 of the sweets in a circle just inside the piped border. Using a small, plain nozzle, pipe another, smaller circle just inside the sweets.

Pipe on the hands of the clock to read the age of the child, e.g. 4 o'clock for a four-year-old, and place the remaining sweet in the centre. Fill in the clock face by piping the sun, moon and stars to represent the 24 hours.

Note: We have based our clock on 24 hours, using one sweet to denote each hour. You can, of course, make it a 12 hour clock by using just 12 sweets, evenly spaced.

CLOCK CAKE *(Photograph: The National Dairy Council)*

CHRISTMAS CELEBRATION

Traditional Golden Turkey
Chestnut Stuffing
Sausage Meat and Celery Stuffing
Roast Potatoes   Cauliflower
Glazed Carrots
Bread Sauce   Cranberry Sauce
Gravy

Crystallized Meringue
Frosted Fruits

Sausage Meat and Celery Stuffing

METRIC/IMPERIAL
25 g/1 oz butter
1 medium onion, chopped
2 sticks celery, finely chopped
500 g/1 lb pork sausage meat
1 tablespoon chopped parsley
1 teaspoon mixed herbs
25 g/1 oz fresh breadcrumbs
salt
freshly ground black pepper

AMERICAN
2 tablespoons butter
1 medium onion, chopped
2 celery stalks, finely chopped
2 cups pork sausage meat
1 tablespoon chopped parsley
1 teaspoon mixed herbs
1/2 cup fresh bread crumbs
salt
freshly ground black pepper

Melt the butter in a frying pan (skillet), add the onion and celery and fry lightly until soft. Remove with a slotted spoon, drain well on kitchen paper towels, then mix with the remaining ingredients, adding salt and black pepper to taste.

Traditional Golden Turkey

METRIC/IMPERIAL
1 × 4.5 kg/10 lb oven-ready turkey
Chestnut Stuffing
Sausage Meat and Celery Stuffing
100 g/4 oz butter, melted
salt
freshly ground black pepper
8 rashers streaky bacon, derinded
To Garnish:
500 g/1 lb chipolatas
225 g/½ lb streaky bacon rashers,
 derinded, and cut in half
bunch of watercress

AMERICAN
1 × 10 lb oven-ready turkey
Chestnut Stuffing
Sausage Meat and Celery Stuffing
½ cup butter, melted
salt
freshly ground black pepper
8 fatty bacon slices, derinded
To Garnish:
1 lb link sausages
½ lb fatty bacon slices, derinded and
 cut in half
bunch of watercress

Remove the giblets from the turkey and use to make stock for gravy. Wipe the turkey inside and out. Stuff the neck end with chestnut stuffing and the body cavity with sausage meat and celery stuffing. Brush the skin with melted butter and season well with salt and pepper. Place in a roasting pan and cover the breast with the bacon. Cook in a preheated moderate oven (160°C/325°F, Gas Mark 3) for 4 hours, basting frequently during cooking.

To prepare the garnish: Place the sausages under a preheated grill (broiler). Roll up the bacon pieces, add to the grill (broiler) pan and return to the grill (broiler). Cook until the sausages are golden and the bacon is crisp. Place the turkey on a large serving dish, surround with the sausages and bacon rolls and garnish with watercress.

Chestnut Stuffing

METRIC/IMPERIAL
3 rashers streaky bacon, derinded and
 chopped
100 g/4 oz fresh white breadcrumbs
1 tablespoon chopped parsley
1 × 225 g/8 oz can chestnut purée
25 g/1 oz butter, melted
salt
freshly ground black pepper
1 egg, beaten

AMERICAN
3 fatty bacon slices, derinded and
 chopped
2 cups fresh white bread crumbs
1 tablespoon chopped parsley
1 × ½ lb can chestnut paste
2 tablespoons butter, melted
salt
freshly ground black pepper
1 egg, beaten

Fry the bacon gently in its own fat until crisp. Remove with a slotted spoon, drain on kitchen paper towels, then mix with the breadcrumbs, parsley, chestnut purée (paste), butter, and salt and black pepper to taste. Mix well and bind with beaten egg.

Bread Sauce

METRIC/IMPERIAL	AMERICAN
1 medium onion	1 medium onion
3 cloves	3 cloves
600 ml/1 pint milk	2½ cups milk
salt	salt
few black peppercorns	few black peppercorns
25 g/1 oz butter	2 tablespoons butter
100 g/4 oz fresh white breadcrumbs	2 cups fresh white bread crumbs

Stud the onion with the cloves. Put in a pan with the milk, salt to taste, and peppercorns, and bring almost to boiling point. Remove from the heat and leave to infuse for 30 minutes.

Remove the peppercorns. Add the butter and breadcrumbs, mix well and cook very gently for 15 minutes, stirring occasionally. Remove the onion, and turn into a jug to serve.

Cranberry Sauce

METRIC/IMPERIAL	AMERICAN
175 g/6 oz sugar	¾ cup sugar
150 ml/¼ pint water	⅔ cup water
225 g/8 oz cranberries	½ lb cranberries
medium sherry (optional)	medium sherry (optional)

Put the sugar and water in a saucepan and heat gently, stirring to dissolve the sugar. Add the cranberries and simmer for about 10 minutes or until the fruit is just soft. Remove from the heat and allow to cool.

If you like, add a little sherry to taste before serving.

Makes about 600 ml/1 pint/2½ cups.

CRYSTALLIZED MERINGUE *(page 90)* ROAST POTATOES,
TRADITIONAL GOLDEN TURKEY *(page 87)*, CAULIFLOWER
(Photograph: The British Poultry Meat Association)

Frosted Fruits

A selection of apples, oranges,
  peaches, plums and grapes
2 egg whites, beaten
sugar

Prepare all the fruits as necessary; make sure they are all quite dry. Dip the fruit into, or brush with, the egg white. Toss in sugar and leave to dry.

Arrange decoratively in a bowl. Serve the same day.

Crystallised Meringue

METRIC/IMPERIAL	AMERICAN
5 egg whites	*5 egg whites*
275 g/10 oz caster sugar	*1⅓ cups superfine sugar*
100 g/4 oz crystallized pineapple, chopped	*¼ lb crystallized pineapple, chopped*
100 g/4 oz glacé cherries, chopped	*½ cup candied cherries, chopped*
25 g/1 oz angelica, chopped	*1 tablespoon angelica, chopped*
50 g/2 oz walnuts, chopped	*½ cup chopped walnuts*
300 ml/½ pint double cream	*1¼ cups heavy cream*
1 tablespoon brandy	*1 tablespoon brandy*
To Decorate:	**To Decorate:**
glacé cherries	*candied cherries*
angelica	*angelica*

Whisk the egg whites until stiff, then whisk in half the sugar, a little at a time. Fold in the remaining sugar.

Spread three quarters of the meringue in a 23 cm/9 inch round on a baking (cookie) sheet lined with non-stick paper or oiled foil.

Put the remaining meringue in a piping (pastry) bag fitted with a plain nozzle and pipe rounds on the edge of the meringue base. Place in a preheated cool oven (140°C/275°F, Gas Mark 1) for 3 to 4 hours until crisp. Place carefully on a serving plate.

Mix the pineapple, cherries, angelica and nuts together and spread over the base of the meringue. Whip the cream with the brandy, put into a piping (pastry) bag and pipe rosettes onto the crystallized fruit. Decorate with cherries and angelica.

INDEX

All-in-one pastry 28
Anna potatoes 70
Apple:
  Apple cheesecake 66
  Harvest crown of lamb 68
  Veal with apples and port
    wine sauce 59
  Waldorf salad 34
Apricot chiffon 76
Avocado:
  Avocado proscuitti 58
  Mexican avocado dip 12

Beef olives with horse-
  radish 39
Biscuits:
  Honey raisin bars 80
  Shortbread animals 82
  Viennese fingers 82
  Oaty chrunchies 78
Black Forest cherry gâteau
  35
Bread sauce 88

Cakes:
  Clock cake 84
  County teapot cake 79
Carrots, glazed 66
Cheese:
  Cheese aigrettes 14
  Cheese fondue 23
  Cheese twists 15
  Gruyère moons 12
  Party kebabs 14
  Tomato surprises 47
  Tuna and cheese flan 31
Cheesecakes:
  Apple Cheesecake 66
  Orange cheesecake 27
  Raspberry cheesecake 75
  Strawberry cheesecake 42
Cherry:
  Black Forest cherry gâteau
    35
Chestnut stuffing 87
Chicken:
  Chicken drum sticks en
    croûte 47
  Mushroom and chicken
    tarts 32
  Pineapple chicken 46
  Polynesian roast chicken 64
Chilled tomato cocktail 19
Chocolate and pear mice 80

Chocolate rum soufflé 62
Choux pastry 52
Cider cup, hot spiced 16
Cider orange cup 22
Clock cake 84
Country teapot cake 79
Crab and lettuce mousse 72
Cranberry sauce 88
Crêpes à l'orange 56
Crystallized meringue 90
Curried macaroni and ham
  salad 54

Desserts:
  Apple Cheesecake 66
  Apricot chiffon 76
  Black Forest cherry gâteau
    35
  Chocolate and pear mice
    80
  Chocolate rum soufflé 62
  Crêpes à l'orange 56
  Crystallized meringue 90
  Fresh fruit flan 28
  Fruit salad 34
  Lemon syllabub 60
  Mandarin pavlovas 71
  Orange cheesecake 27
  Profiteroles 52
  Raspberry cheesecake 75
  Red fruit jelly 51
  Strawberry cheesecake 42
  Strawberry ice cream 70
  Trifle 83
Dip:
  Mexican avocado dip 12
Drinks 16–22
Dubonnet punch 20
Duchess potatoes 74

Egg:
  Stuffed eggs 10

Fish and bacon chowder
  63
Flans see Tarts and flans
Fondue:
  Cheese fondue 23
French dressing 48
Frosted fruits 90
Fruit. See also Apple etc.
  Fresh fruit flan 28
  Frosted fruits 90
  Fruit salad 34

Fruity ginger cup 16
Red fruit jelly 51

Ginger cup, fruity 16
Glazed carrots 66
Grapefruit cups 67
Green salad with vinaigrette
  dressing 40
Gruyère moons 12

Harvest crown of lamb 68
Herb baked tomatoes 56
Honey raisin bars 80
Horseradish, beef olives
  with 39

Ice cream:
  Strawberry ice cream 70

Kebabs:
  Party kebabs 14

Lamb:
  Harvest crown of lamb 68
  Lamb en croûte 74
  Lambs' liver pâté 30
Leeks, seafood with 55
Lemon gin 20
Lemon syllabub 60
Liver:
  Lambs' liver pâté 30

Macaroni and ham salad,
  curried 54
Mandarin pavlovas 71
Mayonnaise 50
Melba toast 44
Mexican avocado dip 12
Mixed salad 50
Moulin rouge 22
Mousse:
  Crab and lettuce mousse
    72
  Smoked haddock mousse
    43
Mulled wine 18
Mushroom:
  Mushroom and chicken
    tarts 32
  Soured cream mushrooms
    36

Orange:
  Cider orange cup 22

INDEX

Crêpes à l'orange 56
Mandarin pavlovas 71
Orange cheesecake 27
Oaty crunchies 78

Party kebabs 14
Party pinwheels 11
Party quiche 44
Pastry:
  All-in-one pastry 28
  Choux pastry 52
Pâté:
  Lambs' liver pâté 30
  Smoked mackerel pâté 38
Pineapple chicken 46
Polynesian roast chicken 64
Potato:
  Anna potatoes 70
  Duchess potatoes 74
  Sugar brown potatoes 60
Prawn:
  Salmon and prawn
    bouchées 11
  Tomato and prawn starter
    24
Profiteroles 52

Quiches see Tarts

Raspberry cheesecake 75
Red fruit jelly 51
Rice:
  Rice salad 48
  Savoury rice 55
Rum cola 20

Salad:
  Fruit salad 34
  Green salad with
    vinaigrette dressing 40
  Mixed salad 50
  Rice salad 48
  Tomato and onion salad 34
  Waldorf salad 34
Salmon and prawn
  bouchées 11
Sauce:
  Bread sauce 88
  Cranberry sauce 88
  Orange sauce 56
  Vegetable sauce 26
Sausage meat and celery
  stuffing 86
Savoury rice 55
Seafood with leeks 55
Sherry sangaree 22
Shortbread animals 82
Shrimp see Prawn
Smoked haddock mousse 43
Smoked mackerel pâté 38
Soufflé:
  Chocolate rum soufflé 62
Soup:
  Fish and bacon chowder 63
Soured cream mushrooms
  36
Strawberry:
  Strawberry cheesecake 42
  Strawberry ice cream 70
  Strawberry wine cup 18
Stuffed eggs 10

Stuffing:
  Chestnut stuffing 87
  Sausage meat and celery
    stuffing 86
Sugar brown potatoes 60
Summer sunset punch 19

Tarts and flans:
  Fresh fruit flan 28
  Mushroom and chicken
    tarts 32
  Party quiche 44
  Tuna and cheese flan 31
Tomato:
  Chilled tomato cocktail 19
  Herb baked tomatoes 56
  Tomato and onion salad
    34
  Tomato and prawn starter
    24
  Tomato surprises 47
Trifle 83
Tuna and cheese flan 31
Turkey:
  Traditional golden
    turkey 87
  Turkey provençal 26

Veal with apples and port
  wine sauce 59
Vegetable sauce 26
Viennese fingers 82
Vinaigrette dressing 40

Waldorf salad 34

The editor would like to thank the following for their assistance in compiling this book:

The Apple & Pear Development Council; British Bacon Bureau; British Poultry Meat Association; British Sugar Bureau; Brown & Polson; Cadbury Typhoo Food Advisory Service; Canned Food Advisory Service; Carlsberg; Cheeses from Switzerland Limited; The Dutch Dairy Bureau; The Dutch Fruit & Vegetable Bureau; Eden Vale; Frank Cooper; Fyffes Group; Green Giant; The Home Baking Bureau; Lea & Perrins; The National Dairy Council; New Zealand Lamb Information Bureau; Stork Cookery Service; Summer Avocados; Taunton Cider; The Tea Council; The White Fish Kitchen

PDO 80-110